JOHN McCRAE

JOHN McCRAE

Beyond Flanders Fields

SUSAN RABY-DUNNE

VICTORIA · VANCOUVER · CALGARY

Heritage House Publishing Company Ltd.

heritagehouse.ca

CATALOGUING INFORMATION AVAILABLE FROM LIBRARY
AND ARCHIVES CANADA

978-1-77203-157-7 (pbk)
978-1-77203-158-4 (epub)
978-1-77203-159-1 (epdf)

Edited by Karla Decker
Proofread by Leslie Kenny
Cover design by Jacqui Thomas
Typesetting by Setareh Ashrafologholai
Cover images: Portrait photo of John Alexander McCrae from *In
Flanders Fields and other Poems by Lieut.-Col. John McCrae, M.D.,
with an Essay in Character*, by Sir Andrew Macphail (New York,
London: G.P. Putnam's Sons, 1919), via Wikimedia Commons;
poppy painting by Sashmir/iStockhoto.com

The interior of this book was produced on 100% post-consumer
recycled paper, processed chlorine free and printed with vegetable-
based inks.

We acknowledge the financial support of the Government of
Canada through the Canada Book Fund (CBF) and the Canada
Council for the Arts, and the Province of British Columbia through
the British Columbia Arts Council and the Book Publishing Tax
Credit.

20 19 18 17 16 1 2 3 4 5

Printed in Canada

In honour of all those who serve,
in memory of all those who fell, and in
mindfulness and compassion for all those
who returned but were forever lost
unto themselves

And for Jack

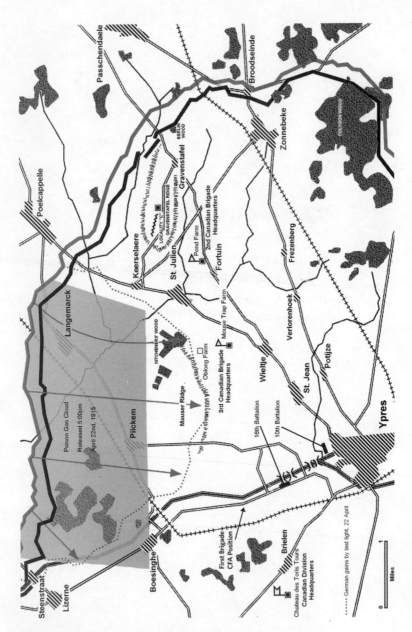

Ypres Salient map with 1st Brigade position. MICHAEL DOROSH, CANADIANSOLDIERS.COM

Contents

Prologue

OF ONE'S FEELINGS ALL THIS NIGHT—*of the asphyxiated French soldiers—of the women and children—of the cheery, steady British reinforcements that moved up quietly past us, going up, not back—I could write, but you can imagine.*

We took to the road at once, and went up at the gallop. The Colonel rode ahead to scout a position (we had only four guns, part of the ammunition column, and the brigade staff; the 1st and 4th batteries were back in reserve at our last billet). Along the roads we went, and made our place on time, pulled up for ten minutes just short of the position, where I put Bonfire with my groom in a farmyard and went forward on foot—only a quarter mile or so—then we advanced. Bonfire had soon to move; a shell killed a horse about four

1

yards away from him, and he wisely took to other ground.
Meantime we went on into the position we were to occupy for
seventeen days, though we could not guess that. I can hardly
say more than that it was near the Yser Canal.

We got into the action at once under heavy gunfire. We
were to the left entirely of the British line, and behind French
troops, and so we remained for eight days. A colonel of the
R.A. [Royal Artillery], known to fame, joined us and camped
with us; he was our link with French Headquarters and was
in local command of the guns in this locality. When he left us
eight days later he said, "I am glad to get out of this hell-hole."

—Excerpt from Major John McCrae's diary of the Second
Battle of Ypres, April 23, 1915

Introduction

JOHN MCCRAE was born into an industrious, enterprising family of Presbyterian Scottish immigrants in Guelph, Ontario, on November 30, 1872. John was the second of three children: brother Tom was the eldest and sister Geills the youngest.

Like his father, Lieutenant-Colonel David McCrae, a long-time member of the artillery militia in Ontario, young John was attracted to military history and objects, particularly guns.

David McCrae was a veteran of the Fenian raids. The Fenians, an Irish Catholic group, many of whom were battle-hardened veterans of the American Civil War, hoped to help free Ireland by attacking British colonial Canada.

For five years, from 1866 to 1871, they raided along the Canadian border from New Brunswick to Manitoba. During the First World War, the elder McCrae raised his own artillery battery, the 43rd, which he planned to command on the field of battle himself; due to his advanced age (seventy-three), that ambition was denied.

As a teenager, John McCrae was an avid reader of the English periodical *The Boy's Own Paper*, a publication filled with swashbuckling tales of British battles and empire-building exploits. The first mention of his fascination with guns was in a letter he wrote at age seven, in which he spoke of watching an artillery competition near his Guelph home: "The Wellington Battery were shooting at the big bench on the Grand River on Saturday. Captain Nicholl made the highest score in the Wellingtons."

David McCrae took John on a business trip to London, England, in 1886. (The family had a woollen mill in Guelph at the time.) McCrae was thirteen and was much impressed by this massive, bustling city at the heart of the British Empire, with its monuments, its history, and its evident prosperity.

On a visit to Edinburgh Castle, McCrae admired the cannons and wrote his mother of one of them, "Saw *Mons Meg*. I could crawl in her mouth easily."

After their return to Canada, McCrae joined the Guelph Highland Cadet Corps once he turned fourteen. He was a keen cadet and applied himself to learning with discipline

Introduction

and dedication. He won a gold medal at age fifteen from the Ontario ministry of education for being the "best-drilled cadet" in Ontario.

He excelled in school, especially in the sciences. From his mother, Janet, he inherited a deep love of literature, poetry, and music. He loved to write and began composing poetry, essays, and short stories in his teens, as well as sketching landscapes. He was a prolific letter and journal writer all his life.

David and Janet McCrae instilled in their three children a strong code of conduct to which they adhered without question. It focused on hard work, fairness, justice, compassion, and a strong belief in service to their church, their fellow men, and their country.

John McCrae loved animals. He had numerous pets at any given time, including a special horse and a dog who would prove to be vital to him in the Great War.

In his later teens, McCrae developed asthma and could not live at Janefield, the family farm on the outskirts of Guelph. He went to stay with a local doctor, and his eventual medical mentor, Doctor Henry Howitt, until he won a science scholarship to the University of Toronto at age seventeen.

John McCrae was a man of his time—a devoted citizen of Canada, but also of the British Empire. So, when the Empire went to war, McCrae did not hesitate to drop everything and sign up—twice.

CHAPTER

1

John McCrae's First War

I see by tonight's bulletin that there is to be no second contingent. I feel sick with disappointment, and do not believe that I have ever been so disappointed in my life, for ever since this business began I am certain there has not been fifteen minutes of my waking hours that it has not been in my mind. It has to come sooner or later. One campaign might cure me, but nothing else ever will, unless it should be old age.

EXCERPT FROM AN 1899 LETTER WRITTEN BY JOHN MCCRAE, REFERRING TO THE UNFOLDING ANGLO-BOER WAR (NOW KNOWN AS THE SECOND BOER WAR, OR THE SOUTH AFRICAN WAR)

BRITAIN HAD ALREADY sown the seeds of conflict in South Africa in the 1880s by annexing the Transvaal and the

Lieutenant John McCrae with artillery column on Metcalfe Street, Ottawa, January 1900. GUELPH MUSEUMS

Orange Free State in the First Boer War. These areas were the domain of the Boers, descendants of Dutch settlers. The Boers were farmers who wanted independence (the word Boer is actually Dutch for farmer). A significant part of this move on the part of the British Empire was to gain more control of the South African gold mines.

When John McCrae wrote the above letter, he was a resident house officer at Johns Hopkins, a new, modern teaching hospital in Baltimore, Maryland. It was a prestigious position. He had recently graduated from the

Lt. John McCrae on Jack. Cape Town, February 1900.
GUELPH MUSEUMS

University of Toronto with honours in medicine. An overall top student, he had won a gold medal for academic excellence. A few of the best medical graduates were selected to come to John Hopkins and study under the brilliant Canadian medical pioneer, William Osler. Osler would become one of McCrae's most important medical mentors.

Yet, when evaluating his residency at Johns Hopkins Hospital against the chance to go to war, he added at the end of the letter quoted above, "My position here I do not regard as an old boot in comparison."

Initially, only a contingent of infantry was sent from Canada to the Second Boer War. In his book *With the*

Guns, E.W.B. (Edward) Morrison, who became friends and served with McCrae in South Africa and later commanded McCrae's artillery brigade in the First World War, spoke of the disappointment:

> All these years we had laboured in camps of instruction in summer and in the armouries during the cold nights of winter, ever stimulated by the hope represented by the will-o-the-wisp of active service ahead of us. Here at last the chance had come, and we were passed over. It was hard to realize it now, but in those days our grief was very real.

According to Morrison, in December 1899, when the British general Redvers Henry Buller was repulsed in a battle at the Tugela River and lost twelve field guns, the need for artillery suddenly became acute. The British sent an urgent request for additional guns and mounted rifles from Canada. John McCrae finally got his wish, and a second contingent of soldiers sailed from Halifax for Cape Town on January 21, 1900, aboard the SS *Laurentian*. McCrae's position at the time was lieutenant leading the right side of D Battery of the Canadian Field Artillery, while Edward Morrison was the lieutenant leading the left side.

Their ship, the SS *Laurentian*, had a nickname, *The Rolling Polly*, the source of which soon became evident as they got into open ocean on the first leg of their voyage to the Cape Verde Islands. In his memoir, Morrison writes, "She swaggered along in a very unladylike style, and then began to try to stand on her head and turn handsprings."

This was an amusing description until one realized the impact on the horses below. Although tended with loving care, nothing could protect them from injuries caused by the continuous pitching of the ship—more deadly in gales—the lack of ventilation, and the stress of their confinement. They died in scores.

After a gale, Morrison reported on the demise of a favourite horse from home:

> Ability, the best charger among the horses brought from Kingston, was bleeding from the nose, and in the afternoon he died. An hour afterwards a steam winch tackle was attached to his remains, and, in the presence of nearly all the men of D Battery who were able to attend the obsequies, the pathetic, limp, sprawling body was jerked into the air and dropped over the side with a great splash. The last seen of Ability, his body was careening sternward over the waves, now a shiny black and now four waving legs above the surf, as the seagulls swooped down and circled about the carcass, with creaky-hinged cries of interrogation. Several hundred sick and white-faced soldiers stood along the troop deck and watched the body shoot by.

McCrae and all the soldiers who loved their horses were heartsick. The voyage to Cape Town was only the first trial the horses were to suffer.

The presence of animals was always a balm for John McCrae's soul, whether he was at home in Canada or on the

Right to left: Edward Morrison on Billy, John McCrae on Jack, Captain Eaton on Amy, Chaplain Cox, and Morrison's servant, Smiddy. Cape Town, February 1900. GUELPH MUSEUMS

field of battle; the Second Boer War was no exception. On the ocean voyage from Canada, D Battery acquired a monkey named Jacko for their mascot. On January 26, while still aboard ship, McCrae noted, "Jacko is getting to be a great nuisance and appears everywhere, making havoc, including chewing the Book of Jeremiah out of Major Hurdman's bible, and various other pranks."

Edward Morrison wrote of Jacko as well, noting, "He got down the Major's field glasses, took them out of the case and is alleged to have been peering out of the porthole with them when apprehended. He has also developed a taste for military literature, and digested portions of the Queen's Regulations and several drill books."

11

The Battery also adopted several dogs, and McCrae spoke affectionately of their bulldog, who made him laugh with his "puffing & grunting & worrying all the time." He spoke fondly of Jack, his horse, who had earned a reputation for "deep thinking by his sober appearance & thoughtful looks." He later wrote, "I shall be sorry to part with the old rascal."

He spoke of the exhausted, undernourished old horse falling asleep on his feet if he was left to stand, and not being urged forward, for even the briefest moments.

Ultimately, if John McCrae was looking for a "cure" for his desire to go to war, it seems this war was not quite it. Due to accidents of timing and placement, and the elusiveness of the enemy, who mostly fought a guerilla-style war, McCrae and his right side of D Battery were involved in only a handful of minor skirmishes. They did not see any action at all until the third week of July, almost six months after they had arrived in South Africa.

The closest John McCrae came to peril was while riding exhausted old Jack through a swamp, when the horse fell on him. McCrae was pinned underneath, and the two of them very nearly drowned before being hauled out. He had ridden back and forth through the gumbo several times while supervising his column's laboured crossing of the swollen, swampy Olifants Vlei River on the march to Kenhardt—there were supply wagons, limbers (special wagons for hauling field guns), men on foot, and men on horses.

The condition of the horses was notoriously bad due to inadequate feed and water and the heavy physical demands placed on them. They were a constant source of anxiety for McCrae. He was criticized for being overly careful with the horses and mules, but in the end he was praised. His battery lost far fewer horses than other units, due expressly to McCrae's care for them and his constant efforts to secure proper feed and water.

His inherent sense of fair play suffered an affront on April 3, 1900. He wrote his mother, "740 men here—75 cases of dysentery. The staff (meaning the British officers) have commandeered all the water tanks in town; as a result the staff are actually washing in clear water, while the Canadians, officers & men, have to drink the muddy river water. Then to add insult to injury the staff surgeon—a civilian—named Sherwin, from nobody knows where—comes down & rides around & says, 'You d___ fools, don't drink that water.'"

If there were any highlights at all for him, they had to do with legendary characters that he met personally, including author Rudyard Kipling and the famous British field marshal, Lord Frederick Roberts of Kandahar. The camaraderie and the friendships he made, most notably with Edward Morrison, and his deep appreciation of the natural beauty of the land and wildlife of South Africa were positive experiences as well.

He first met Rudyard Kipling near the beginning of his tour of duty, in the Mount Nelson Hotel in Cape

Town, along with Edward Morrison and their battery chaplain, J.W. Cox. McCrae excitedly wrote to his mother about meeting "the High Priest of it all." He reported that they had

> five minutes chat. He told us a few things about up country. He is charmingly free and easy—says up country is <u>Hell</u>. Asked a good deal about our corps. Said that he had been up in camp but thought from our appearance that we were not receiving. He was dressed in Kharkee, is short & rather round faced—with the glasses on as usual. We were all delighted to meet him.

He wrote that Kipling's parting words to them "were to boil their water, and fine any man who does not." This turned out to be excellent advice and was taken to heart by McCrae.

Later, while in the field after their first skirmish on July 21 at De Wagendrift, McCrae and D Battery were inspected by Lord Roberts. Roberts asked to meet the officers, and when they were called out, McCrae stepped forward, relishing the chance to shake hands with another of his long-time heroes.

Most of John McCrae's activities in the Second Boer War consisted of interminable, seemingly pointless marches— he reckoned they had marched upwards of eight hundred miles (about thirteen hundred kilometres), all told—in desolate, inhospitable scrublands. They drilled and drilled, and guarded railway lines. But at almost every town they came to, the enemy had gotten wind of their approach and vanished.

More Canadian soldiers died of exposure, bad water, and disease exacerbated by filthy conditions than in battle. This may have been the beginning of McCrae's disdain for the Canadian Army Medical Corps. He wrote to his father on May 20, 1900, "I am glad I am not a med[ical officer] out here: no thank you. No R[oyal] A[rmy] M[edical] C[orps] or any other M[edical] C[orps] for me."

When he saw the condition of one of the so-called hospitals, he was disgusted by the terrible sanitation, stating, "for absolute neglect and rotten administration, it is a model."

McCrae did attend kindly and efficiently to the medical needs of his men, even though this was not in his job description as an artillery lieutenant. He was very popular with his fellow officers and subordinates alike. He was funny and full of stories, songs, and laughter. He had a way of being familiar and down to earth with the men he commanded, while still enjoying their respect.

Edward Morrison writes of McCrae in his 1901 memoir *With the Guns*: "Lieutenant McCrae is of a philosophic turn of mind, and has a love for the curious and unique in art and nature. He is engaged in making a collection of gems of profanity, scintillations of genius evoked by the conditions and trials of war upon the Canadian intellect."

In Pretoria, just before they set off for Cape Town and the voyage home, McCrae and several other officers and gunners came down with a fever, and he was briefly hospitalized. There was some doubt as to whether he'd make the sailing home.

Morrison wrote in his memoir, "The gunners all hope Mr. McCrae will get down in time, for we all like Jack." McCrae did recover in time to sail with his mates, and the soldiers of D Battery arrived home to a heroes' welcome on January 9, 1901.

When McCrae was welcomed by the mayor of Guelph, it was reported that he remarked, with typical humility, "For myself I have nothing to say, but I do feel like paying tribute to the unselfish and soldierly qualities of the men whom I had the honour to command."

Shortly after his return from South Africa, John McCrae left the uniform behind and boarded a train for McGill University in Montreal. For the present, he would resume his medical profession.

Montreal, 1900–1914

McCrae was a man of great dignity and great culture whose bedside clinics in physical diagnosis were interspersed with classical quotations and whose English had a poetic cadence. To me he imparted a feeling for the human side of medicine. Aloofness, excessive dignity, superiority and frock coats were the common defences for the medical ignorance of some of his colleagues; with McCrae it was humility and compassion.

EXCERPT FROM THE MEMOIR *SMALL PATIENTS: AUTOBIOG-RAPHY OF A CHILDREN'S DOCTOR*, BY ALTON GOLDBLOOM (JOHN MCCRAE'S STUDENT)

AFTER THE BOER WAR, McCrae went to live, study, teach, and work in Montreal, which, at the turn of the century,

Sir William Osler and Lady Grace Osler (in white); John McCrae
to the left of William; Tom McCrae to the right of Grace; and "Ike"
Edward Revere Osler perched on the railing. Murray Bay, Quebec,
August 1904. OSLER LIBRARY MCGILL UNIVERSITY

had at its centre a wealthy, English-speaking hub of finance,
industry, shipping, and manufacturing. Montreal's influ-
ential people lived in stately, opulent homes on the lower
slopes of Mount Royal, adjacent to McGill University—a
district referred to in later years as the "Square Mile," or the
"Golden Square Mile."

Because John McCrae was now a decorated veteran and
physician who counted among his mentors such prominent
medical pioneers as William Osler and Osler's McGill suc-
cessor, J.G. (George) Adami, he was soon rubbing shoulders

with the Montreal elite. Often sought as a dinner guest at homes such as that of the Molsons of brewing fame, or Lord Strathcona's, he cut a handsome figure in his military dress uniform. His good looks and expertise as a raconteur made him a very popular figure of the time.

At McGill, McCrae and George Adami were kindred spirits who shared a love of learning, art, literature, and travel. Both were witty, cultured men who had a talent for making numerous and lifelong friends.

As a physician, McCrae had learned from William Osler a general style and bedside manner of familiarity and kindness. Osler was known to joke with patients and touch them with a comforting hand: a pat on the shoulder, or a squeeze of the foot.

As a medical teacher, McCrae had a talent for engaging students with liberal doses of humour and making difficult subjects interesting and understandable for all. His weekly early-morning pathology demonstrations were so popular that students rarely missed them. He relied on case studies that were as varied as they were fascinating. Discussions of how findings were arrived at were delivered in such a colourful way that students did not forget them.

George Adami had this to say about McCrae the teacher:

John McCrae was a born teacher. His demonstrations were impressive, and sharp was his criticism, each point being made with a snap which reminded one that he was a student of Carlyle [Thomas Carlyle, Scottish philosopher of the 1800s]. . . . The students loved him for the interest he always displayed in their difficulties and because he showed the human side of medicine . . . They loved him, too, because he never feared to step from the dignity of the teacher to the level of the student."

McCrae was a Governor's Fellow in Pathology and by 1902 had performed some 417 autopsies at Montreal General Hospital; most of the people had died of typhoid or tuberculosis. He also conducted research in McGill's pathology laboratories.

From 1903 to 1912, McCrae served as a visiting professor at the University of Vermont in Burlington, teaching bacteriology and pathology. Two Wednesdays a month, on his day off, he would take the train from Montreal to Burlington and back, arriving home late in the evening.

McCrae continued his hobby of dabbling in poetry, and in 1904 one of his poems was published in *The McGill University Magazine*. The poem was titled "Upon Watts' Picture 'Sic Transit'":

"What I spent, I had; what I saved, I lost; what I gave, I have."

But yesterday the tourney, all the eager joy of life,
    The waving of the banners, and the rattle of the spears,
The clash of sword and harness, and the madness of the strife;

To-night begin the silence and the peace of endless years.

(One sings within.)

But yesterday the glory and the prize,
    And best of all, to lay it at her feet,
To find my guerdon in her speaking eyes:
    I grudge them not,—they pass, albeit sweet.

The ring of spears, the winning of the fight,
    The careless song, the cup, the love of friends,
The earth in spring—to live, to feel the light—
    'Twas good the while it lasted: here it ends.

Remain the well-wrought deed in honour done,
    The dole for Christ's dear sake, the words that fall
In kindliness upon some outcast one,—
    They seemed so little: now they are my All.

In Watts's painting, a knight lies on a slab, covered by a shroud. Alongside the slab are his shield, spear, a mandolin, a book, peacock feathers, and other objects. Across the wall above are the words "What I spent, I have, What I saved, I lost, What I gave, I have." Watts spent a lot of time musing about death and the meaning and purpose of human existence. John McCrae also concerned himself with these things, and almost all of his poetry reflected this. His poems were often sombre creations showing a preoccupation with death and what comes after. This dark preoccupation was unexpected because it was so completely at odds with his cheery demeanour and obvious enthusiasm for life and learning.

In these early years at McGill, McCrae kept up with the artillery militia somewhat, but as he got busier and busier, he stopped being involved, simply for the lack of time. He did, however, always make time to attend St. Paul's Presbyterian Church.

In 1904 he was invited by the University of Vermont to give the opening address to the medical faculty at the beginning of the school year, a singular honour for such a young man—McCrae was thirty-four years old. He titled his presentation "The Privileges of Medicine." The gist of his talk, coloured throughout by his Christian beliefs, was that it was the duty of doctors to serve all patients, whether rich or poor, with devotion and to the best of their ability.

A paragraph from the address illuminates his philosophy:

> It will be in your power every day to store up for yourself treasure that will come back to you in the consciousness of duty well done, of kind acts performed; things that having given away freely, you yet possess.

Two years later, in 1906, McCrae published another poem in *The McGill University Magazine*. Titled "The Unconquered Dead," this poem related to his experience in the Boer War. Again the theme was death, the dead, and peace after death. (This was the first of McCrae's three war poems most closely related in theme; the next was "In

Flanders Fields," which was followed by the last poem he
ever wrote, "The Anxious Dead."

Here is "The Unconquered Dead":

" . . . defeated, with great loss."

Not we the conquered! Not to us the blame
    Of them that flee, of them that basely yield;
Nor ours the shout of victory, the fame
    Of them that vanquish in a stricken field.

That day of battle in the dusty heat
    We lay and heard the bullets swish and sing
Like scythes amid the over-ripened wheat,
    And we the harvest of their garnering.

Some yielded, No, not we! Not we, we swear
    By these our wounds; this trench upon the hill
Where all the shell-strewn earth is seamed and bare,
    Was ours to keep; and lo! we have it still.

We might have yielded, even we, but death
    Came for our helper; like a sudden flood
The crashing darkness fell; our painful breath
    We drew with gasps amid the choking blood.

The roar fell faint and farther off, and soon
    Sank to a foolish humming in our ears,
Like crickets in the long, hot afternoon
    Among the wheat fields of the olden years.

Before our eyes a boundless wall of red
    Shot through by sudden streaks of jagged pain!
Then a slow-gathering darkness overhead
    And rest came on us like a quiet rain.

Not we the conquered! Not to us the shame,
    Who hold our earthen ramparts, nor shall cease
To hold them ever; victors we, who came
    In that fierce moment to our honoured peace.

McCrae was pleased when he was invited to join an exclusive group known as the Pen and Pencil Club. They met every two weeks in the upstairs studio of Montreal artist Edmond Dyonnet, and members included humourist Stephen Leacock, *McGill University Magazine* editor Andrew Macphail, classicist John Macnaughton, the Canadian Pacific Railway builder William Van Horne, and others. It was said, jokingly, to be a "drinking club," and Leacock remarked that members were permitted, with some reluctance, to read their literary efforts.

In the middle of all this, McCrae fell in love with a woman, whose name he would never reveal, from a prominent Montreal family. He called her Lady R, or his "esteemed lady." When she went to New York, McCrae hoped against hope that she would return to Montreal and give him a chance. When he received word that she was not coming back, he wrote his colleague and close McGill friend, Oskar Klotz, confessing that she had left him "with a choice between suicide and work."

In a scrapbook in the Osler Library at McGill, there is a letter from the mystery woman to Billy Turner, another close friend and medical colleague of McCrae's. In the letter she speaks disparagingly of McCrae's habit of wearing old, usually too-small suits. Andrew Macphail had noted in the margin of the letter, "And this is the darling McCrae was in love with until his death."

In 1910, McCrae was invited as an expedition doctor on an exciting adventure with Canada's Governor General, Earl Grey. They set off in several canoes on a journey of three thousand miles (just under five thousand kilometres) from Norway House, at the northeast corner of Lake Winnipeg, to York Factory and Churchill in Hudson Bay, and then on to Baffin Island, returning via the east coast of Cape Breton to the St. Lawrence River, where they boarded the steamship *Earl Grey* for the return trip to Montreal. The trip took a month and was full of wonder for McCrae, who loved the outdoors and revelled in the welcome break from his intensive doctor's schedule. He was especially moved by some Indigenous people he met near the start of the journey, whose traditions he found fascinating. Leo Amery, an English journalist and eventual British member of parliament, was on board, and in his 1940 memoir, *Days of Fresh Air*, spoke of McCrae: "As a story teller I've never met his equal, and every night in our mess tent, or round the campfire he would pour out his anecdotes, and never repeated himself."

* * *

McCrae returned to McGill and his usual hectic schedule. By 1913 he was doing rounds at three Montreal hospitals, running a private practice, lecturing as a professor of pathology, publishing medical research papers, and working hard on *A Text-Book of Pathology*, a comprehensive work he co-authored with George Adami and launched in June 1914.

In "An Essay in Character" (1919), Sir Andrew Macphail wrote of McCrae's work ethic:

> It is all disclosed in his words, "I have never refused any work that was given me to do." These records are merely a chronicle of work. Outdoor clinics, laboratory tasks, post-mortems, demonstrating, teaching, lecturing, attendance upon the sick in wards and homes, meetings, conventions, papers, addresses, editing, reviewing—the very remembrance of such a career is enough to appall the stoutest of hearts.
>
> But John McCrae was never appalled. He went about his work gaily, never busy, never idle. Each minute was pressed into the service and every hour was made to count.

Then, to add to all of this industry, it was said by several colleagues that in the odd half hour, he found the time to write poetry.

At the end of the 1914 school year, John McCrae and his friends, particularly those in the militia, discussed with interest and more than a little anxiety the assassination of Archduke Franz Ferdinand and his wife on June 28 in Sarajevo. This could not be good, and where would it lead? McCrae's busy schedule did not allow him to fret over it too much, but he kept an eye on the papers.

* * *

In August 1914, McCrae was on the ship *Scotian*, heading for a holiday in England and a visit with the Oslers. (William Osler had left Johns Hopkins for an appointment as dean of medicine at Oxford.) Eight days out, McCrae received word that England had declared war on Germany. He wrote to his brother, Tom, on August 5: "Surely good old emperor Billy has got his head in the noose at last: it is now he or us, good and well. It will be a terrible war, and somebody's finish when all is said and done . . . I'm afraid my holiday trip is knocked 'galley west.' However, we shall see."

McCrae stayed only briefly in London. His old friend Edward Morrison, now commander of the 1st Brigade Canadian Field Artillery, cabled him there, offering McCrae a dual position: major, second-in-command, and brigade surgeon. On September 9, McCrae wrote to his sister Geills: "Out on the awful old trail again! And with very mixed feelings, but some determination. I am off to Valcartier tonight. I was really afraid to go home, and afraid it would only be harrowing for Mater, and I think she agrees. My add [address] will be Major McC, 1st Bgde Fd Arty, Valcartier, PQ."

Many of McCrae's McGill friends and colleagues would serve in the First World War, including surgeon Francis Scrimger, later to win the Victoria Cross in the Second Battle of Ypres; Andrew Macphail, who would command the 6th Field Ambulance from Locre, at the foot of Mont Kemmel in Belgium; and Edward Archibald, Canada's first neurosurgeon, in whose house McCrae had rented an apartment for eight years.

The buildup to the war had been years in the making, following decades of militarization, political manoeuvring, and shifting alliances among the economic powers of Europe and Western Asia. When Archduke Ferdinand, an ally of Germany, was murdered by the terrorist Gavrilo Princip—a member of the Young Bosnia group and of the secret military society the Black Hand—it seemed as though a small Balkan War was about to ignite. But within a couple of weeks, like a match to a fuse, a chain of terrible repercussions was set in motion, and what had initially a looked like local a skirmish soon escalated into the terrible conflagration that became the First World War.

With England, France, and Russia allied in their Triple Entente (signed in 1907), Germany was isolated and surrounded by perceived enemies. The country was already hostile toward and envious of the British Empire's vast domain. When German soldiers mobilized and marched into neutral Belgium, the British issued an ultimatum.

Germany was to withdraw from Belgium, and they were to respond to Britain by midnight on August 4. The deadline came and went. Just after midnight on August 5, 1914, Britain was at war with Germany.

Canada Prepares
for War

The Army Medical Corps men say—I apologize—I am too good a man to waste on the firing line. I am afraid nothing is too good for this firing line.

EXCERPT FROM A LETTER FROM JOHN MCCRAE,
AT VALCARTIER, TO HIS MOTHER, SEPTEMBER 19, 1914

IT WASN'T LONG before a wave of enthusiasm for war swept the Commonwealth countries. Canada, with its large population of immigrants from England, Scotland, and Ireland, was particularly keen.

A suggestion was made to make the existing base at Petawawa, Ontario, the main centre for enlistment and

Lieutenant-Colonel William Dodds and Major John McCrae at Camp Valcartier, September 1914. UNIVERSITY OF VICTORIA

training. The brash, blustering Sam Hughes, minister of the militia, ignored that suggestion because he believed Petawawa was too far from shipping access; he put the wheels in motion to build a training camp in Valcartier, Quebec, on the Jacques Cartier River. Valcartier was only fourteen miles (twenty-three kilometres) from Quebec City and the St. Lawrence River, where troopships could be conveniently filled and sent off to England.

Choosing to build the training camp at Valcartier was one of the better decisions made by the controversial Minister Hughes, who was known to be overbearing and— some said—a martial maniac. He would oversee Canada's war for the next two and a half years. Constantly embroiled in one scandal or another, many to do with his preference for awarding lucrative contracts to his cronies, Hughes revelled in being the centre of attention.

Edward Morrison wrote of Sam Hughes in his memoir, *The War as Morrison Saw It*:

> Knowing him as long as I had I must admit that I was prepared to number him among the maniacs with the numerous other critics of the minister of the militia, when he one day announced he was going to raise, commission and immediately train and equip 33,000 troops of all arms, and transport them at once to the seat of war.

Sam Hughes did achieve the seemingly impossible, in just under six weeks, by taking charge of the Valcartier wilderness, getting it cleared, and turning it into a thriving military training camp that initially housed twenty thousand troops, and eventually more than thirty-six thousand.

John McCrae returned from England and was delighted to catch up at Valcartier with Lieutenant-Colonel Edward Morrison and his old artillery pals. He hoped to serve with them again, although early on he said he would serve wherever he was put. But he also made comments about not wanting to be in the medical corps, whose members he had described in a letter to his mother as a "queer lot."

At Valcartier, a sea of white bell tents soon sprang up. With its mess buildings, electricity, roads, latrines, and telephone lines, it was a small city, carved out of the wilderness in record time.

Canada had never been involved in anything like this, and everyone was flying by the seat of their pants. They made up rules and procedures as they went along.

John McCrae was kept busy examining and "attesting" soldiers as fit or unfit for duty. He performed hundreds of inoculations. On September 19, 1914, he wrote to his mother, "Work goes on briskly: we spend our days from 5:30 until 9 fairly continuously, I assure you. Today I went over about 100 men for their descriptions etc. and have still a lot left."

McCrae was issued a mount that proved to be unsatisfactory. The horse stumbled a lot and couldn't keep up with Colonel Morrison's horse, King.

McCrae's horse problems were soon remedied when McGill tropical-medicine specialist Doctor John Todd and his equestrian wife, Marjorie, made McCrae a present of one of the finest hunter-jumpers from their stable. They wanted their friend to have a solid, reliable mount and felt they could contribute in this practical way to the war effort. Named Bonfire, the horse was a substantial, Irish-type thoroughbred. Big and beautiful at 16.2 hands, a bright chestnut the colour of burnished copper, with sparkling white socks, he turned out to have just as sparkling a personality. McCrae wrote to his mother, "I got my horse here today: He looks very promising . . . one of these chaps that 'nuzzles' into your chest on slight provocation. He and my present one are side by side." So began a treasured relationship that took on more importance and gravity for McCrae as time passed.

When they were ready to set sail for England, the 30,617 men of the First Canadian Contingent, along with seven thousand horses, marched down to thirty-three waiting ships on the St. Lawrence River in the port of Quebec City. McCrae and his entire 1st Brigade, with all of their guns, wagons, and horses, were assigned to the troopship SS *Saxonia*.

Eventually, all were boarded, and the contingent departed Quebec on October 3, 1914. All the ships gathered along the Gaspé Peninsula before setting out across the open ocean. They moved into the Atlantic in three columns of eleven ships. Each column was escorted by British battleships, seven in all. There was a prevailing atmosphere of enthusiasm on board the ships; most of these young Canadians were naively unprepared for the carnage that was coming. Many would never see their Canadian homes again.

The passage to England was smooth for the first twelve days, but a terrific storm blew up just at the end. There was much vomiting overboard and in other, less convenient places. The horses in the hold suffered most, and many were knocked around, bruised, and battered before the storm calmed. The ships were supposed to land at Portsmouth, but due to rumours of U-boats in that area, they detoured west to Plymouth.

John McCrae and his comrades in the 1st Brigade CFA (Canadian Field Artillery) were lucky to have their own ship, given the chaos that ensued when it was time for the thousands of soldiers to disembark at Plymouth.

4

On Salisbury Plain

It is now 5:45 and I am writing in the orderly tent—the rain pelting and the wind blowing, and all this time feeling that if one is comfortable enough himself, the horses are not.

EXCERPT FROM JOHN MCCRAE'S PERSONAL WAR DIARY,
ON SALISBURY PLAIN, DECEMBER 7, 1914

TO SAY THAT there was chaos upon arrival would be an understatement. While the British may have welcomed the idea of a horde of Canadian colonials coming to help with their war effort, in practical terms they were wholly unprepared.

Lieutenant-Colonel Edward Morrison later reported that there was immediately a clash of orders from the British navy and the port authority. First, his brigade was ordered to stay aboard the SS *Saxonia* pending receipt of a written order from a certain high-ranking officer in the port. An armed guard was stationed at the bottom of the gangway to ensure no member of the brigade could leave the ship.

Shortly after that, a curt naval officer came on board, ignored the Canadian officer in charge of the guard, and proceeded to order that every man, horse, and bit of equipment be off the ship by nightfall.

The Canadian captain of the guard politely explained that he would be happy to do this, but he had express orders from a senior port officer to stay put.

The naval officer flew into a rage and suggested that these half-trained Canucks did not know what their duty was. The captain calmly replied that they knew enough to carry out a written order. The naval officer came back with a threat that if they did not disembark forthwith, a force of armed sailors would be dispatched to take them off. Shortly after that, about two hundred armed sailors gathered on the dock and prepared to enforce the naval officer's wishes.

Eventually, the naval officer and the port authority got their information aligned, but there was no explanation or apology of any sort to the Canadians. The brigade stayed put, and, late into the night, a cancellation order finally arrived from the original port authority. It is easy to imagine what sort of taste this left in the mouths of the Canadians, who had travelled such a long distance to serve King and Empire. It was not a happy start.

The huge crowds of curious well-wishers, eager to get a look at these men from the wilds of Canada, had added to the chaos at Plymouth Harbour. When the Canadians finally began to disembark, the onlookers handed the men fruit, candies, and cigarettes by way of welcome.

Altogether it took some nine days to get everyone off the boats and onto land. The soldiers at the end of the line were understandably stir-crazy by the time they disembarked. Then came the matter of feeding, housing, and providing shelter for this mass of men, horses, and equipment.

The 1st Brigade CFA got all of them onto a train at Plymouth station, and off they went across Devon, travelling five or six hours in the dark before detraining. They were cheered the whole way by thousands of country people and villagers. Once detrained, they marched the rest of the night across Salisbury Plain to their camp, arriving at sunrise. Just before dawn, they found themselves marching by that strange and otherworldly collection of upright stones known as Stonehenge. After seeing to the horses, the men threw themselves down in empty tents and fell fast asleep.

When they got up later that day, the brigade realized immediately that Valcartier had been a model of preparedness compared to Salisbury Plain and the wide-open, windswept West Down North Camp, which would become their home for most of the next four months. They could not have imagined that it would be almost six months before they would be brought into the theatre of war.

On Salisbury Plain

Salisbury Plain was an established British artillery training area. It should have been a perfect location for training and drilling horse teams and their drivers, gunners and their guns, and those with support duties. It should have been, but it was not. Between the time the Canadians arrived and Christmas 1914, it rained every day for seven solid weeks. Out of 123 days that fall and winter on Salisbury Plain, it rained for 89 of them. And because a layer of chalk lay underneath the scant topsoil, the rain was not absorbed but instead accumulated on top of the ground.

Horses tied in lines began to fail from exposure and hoof-rot, an equine version of trench foot. McCrae and the officers were able to secure materials to make decent shelters for their personal mounts. But the horses that pulled the limbers (part of a gun carriage) and the wagon horses suffered severe, sometimes deadly hypothermia in the relentless rains and wind.

McCrae reported in his diary on the afternoon of November 18, 1914, that his hands were so cold they were actually painful. Too cold to stay in their tents, the officers could at least go into the orderly room, which had a stove, and their woollen greatcoats added warmth. McCrae noted that the men were much worse off, and lice were rife. Their tents became filthy because nothing was ever dry. Altogether, the conditions were horrible for men and horses.

The food was not as good as at Valcartier, either. Even that would have kept soldiers somewhat happy.

Adding to this misery, information was heavily cen-
sored. The Canadians received no reports of what was
happening in France and no word as to when they would
likely be sent over.

McCrae reported that there was a standing order on
Salisbury Plain: "Picketing of horses in plantations is prohibited." In other words, they could not tie horses up in any
of the woods surrounding the open plain, which would have
offered at least some shelter from the elements. McCrae
wrote in his journal on November 19, "These orders are
standing . . . I suppose since the year 1200 A D, and it seems
to me, might well at this time be suspended."

McCrae spent significant amounts of time attending to
sick parades of long lines of men. The cold and damp lent
itself to continuous colds, influenza, and chest complaints,
although nothing too serious—yet.

On November 23, a welcome visitor appeared in camp:
Rudyard Kipling. John McCrae and Edward Morrison were
excited to meet with their hero for the first time since Cape
Town. He came back to lunch with the brigade the following
day. McCrae wrote that he was "chatty and interested—
excellent company. He carries his age very well & looks far
less than his years. He has a son in the Irish Guards who is
presently at the front."

Kipling was interested in an order the brigade had
received from British staff headquarters. The brigade had

been advised that a certain resident riding his horse on his *private training gallop* on the plain was being inconvenienced by gun-wheel ruts created during the brigade's drill practices. The man was concerned about the potential for injury. The brigade was told to take pains to keep out of that area. McCrae commented, "What a piece of truly Britannic foolishness!"

The brigade continued to drill when the weather permitted, which was not very often. At the end of November, McCrae, Lieutenant-Colonel Morrison, and Colonel William Dodds rode to Lark Hill, where construction was started on huts to get the men out of the damp tents. The huts were not roomy, and it looked as though the men would be squeezed together even more than they already were. McCrae noted tersely, "No sign as yet of horse shelters."

On St. Andrew's Day, McCrae and Dodds were told dinner would be a little special that evening. The first thing on the bill of fare was Scotch broth. McCrae said it "smelt so high, no one dared tackle it."

A couple of nights later, McCrae was in his cot and heard a questioning voice outside. "I called, Kitty, and a beautiful grey cat came in through a slit in the door of the tent. She promptly made herself at home on another cot." This delighted him, and he added, "I wish had had a dog or a pet of some sort, though again I don't; war isn't any place for pets."

That night there was a terrific storm, the worst the brigade had yet experienced. The wind seemed to be blowing from every direction, and some tents were pulled down or completely apart. The brigade put their horses in the woods for shelter. Then someone from HQ came out at night and made them take them out again.

McCrae felt that the entire brigade was very fit and ready, if only the horses had shelter. This was an increasingly pressing issue as more brigade horses failed due to the cold and standing in water day and night. Bonfire was a little lame due to a piece of chalk in his shoe, but he soon got over it and was frisky again.

The state of the horses became a constant preoccupation; an artillery brigade was utterly dependent upon them. Both Morrison and McCrae put forward continual requests for horse shelters but were met only with silence. "It is really pitiful and it makes me boil," wrote McCrae in his journal on December 6.

The last straw came when the Canadians discovered that the nearby woods were preserved for fox hunting. "We are doing our duty as best we see it, but it is heartbreaking."

Meanwhile, many soldiers were sick, and McCrae had to attend to them, sometimes slogging four or five hundred yards through deep, sticky mud. He tried not to let the weather get him down, but it was the worst he had ever experienced, and he was certainly not alone in feeling this. He believed a lot of the men were sick simply because they had lost heart. The whole Salisbury Plain exercise seemed like an ongoing and pointless nightmare.

Finally, the senior officers of the 1st Brigade CFA arranged to rent a nearby property, New Copse Farm, at their own expense. Once they got all their horses into the barns and shelters there, the horses immediately began to recover. The British staff also relented on the rule about picketing horses in the woods and finally allowed it. But the 1st Brigade was only too happy to have its own stables at last.

The officers did get a break regularly and made the nearby Bear Inn in Devizes their officers' mess. There is no way to overstate how wonderful a break that was for John McCrae, and for Bonfire, too. While the officers refreshed themselves, their horses were stabled in relatively luxurious stalls with fresh straw for bedding and hay and oats to eat for a change.

On December 17, John McCrae rode to the town of Lavington with a young lieutenant in the brigade named Alexis Helmer. They had met briefly in the militia in Quebec. Helmer was a graduate of civil engineering at McGill and also of the Royal Military College in Kingston, Ontario, as an artillery officer. He was a popular young fellow in the brigade, and his name would go down in history once they got into battle near Ypres, Belgium.

Christmas Eve came, and McCrae and two other officers cooked a turkey, a goose, spuds, Brussels sprouts, plum pudding, and mince pies. They could at least create a little home away from home with a Christmas feast. Later that evening, he learned a couple of brigade men were in the guard tent after causing a disturbance in Bath. It being Christmas Eve, McCrae popped by with a bottle of "medicine" for each man with the handwritten words on the label, To Be Taken Before Meals. He had brought each a measure of rum.

While on an excursion, McCrae reported on January 9, 1915, "Bonfire made the biggest exhibition I have ever seen him make over—a pig! I could not get him within 50 yards of it, and he will walk past a smoking traction engine . . . he gave no explanation of what kind of a wild beast he thought it was."

After having been kept in the dark about operations in France and when they might deploy, and feeling battered and beaten by the terrible weather, the brigade was further demoralized by a speech delivered by Lord Kitchener in the first week of January. Kitchener stated that they were not trained well enough for any of the six armies. His words gave the suggestion that their British commanding officer, Lieutenant-General Edwin Alderson, had put them in this position through his lack of knowledge of his troops. The brigade men were knocked flat by these remarks, and many were indignant. Colonel Morrison found the comments unacceptable. He had served with Alderson in South Africa and had a high degree of respect for his competence.

The men carried on as well as they could, drilling when the weather permitted. McCrae began giving hundreds of typhoid inoculations, including one to himself, which caused an unfavourable reaction—pain and a terrible night's sleep.

The huts for the men were finally finished on Lark Hill, and the men moved out of their tents. They would have been better off if they'd stayed in them. They were now in cramped quarters with poor ventilation, and the result was an epidemic of meningitis. Tragically, twenty-eight young men died of the disease.

The weather picked up in January, and they were able to have some good, full days of artillery drill. They had some extra excitement when an "aeroplane" flew over and then crashed into the side of a hill right in front of them. Several men ran to help, but, miraculously, before they could get there the pilot crawled out unharmed.

As January came to an end, they finally got word they would be leaving soon for France. This lifted everyone's spirits. Indeed, the soldiers had often stated they would rather be on a firing line any day than stuck on Salisbury Plain in the terrible weather, seemingly to no purpose.

Bonfire had a little attack of colic but got over it quickly. Meanwhile, McCrae busied himself with continuing to administer typhoid inoculations to lines of soldiers from all brigades and regiments.

He enjoyed a brief respite with Captain Cosgrave when they went to a dance at the local town hall. McCrae danced with a Mrs. Anderson, whom he had met on the SS *Scotian* in the summer. He was suddenly called out of the dance at 10:30 and asked if he could attend to someone nearby who had taken poison. The patient turned out to be a civilian who had not taken poison but had become delusional and thought townspeople were trying to poison him. He'd gotten hold of a meat axe and was smashing up windows and whatever else he could swing at. McCrae got the police involved, by which time the dance was over, and he was off to bed earlier than he would have liked.

The last couple of weeks on the Plain, the brigade had the luxury of billeting in and around Devizes—the officers, of course, in their mess at the Bear Inn. Bonfire was undoubtedly happy to be in a comfy stall for a while. McCrae spent the last few days going through his "war kit," trying to streamline it as much as possible. He sent the excess to Sir William Osler's home in Oxford.

The last "sick parade" before departure took place on February 7. McCrae gave his final series of inoculations. Five men refused the inoculations and were sent home. McCrae thought they probably had cold feet and that it was better to find out now than on the battlefield.

Colonel Morrison thought the brigade to be well drilled by departure time and was confident they were ready for

Major John McCrae (bottom left), Col. Edward Morrison (bottom centre), Col. William Dodds (bottom 6th right), Capt. Lawrence Cosgrave (bottom 3rd right), and Lieutenant Alexis Helmer (top 5th left), at the Bear Hotel in Devizes, England, 1915. CANADIAN WAR MUSEUM

battle. Orders to leave England were greeted with the greatest enthusiasm by every gunner in the brigade.

At dawn on February 7, the men of the 1st Brigade CFA travelled by train from Devizes to Avonmouth, on the coast, where they boarded the ship that would take them to France. Bonfire got to luxuriate in a comfortable padded horsebox. By dinnertime they—three hundred men and two hundred and fifty horses—were on board the *African Prince* under the command of Captain Pierce. There were only six three-man cabins for the officers. McCrae and Morrison took one. They would sail for France early on the morning of February 8.

They did not realize it, but these were to be their last days of peace, in many cases forever. Half of the men would never return to Canada.

5

Neuve-Chapelle

*I attend to the gun lines; any casualty is reported by telephone
and I go to it ... It is not nice to come upon a pool of blood, because one speculates just what kind of knock the chap got, and
so on ... Most of the trench injuries are of the head [sniper
shots], and therefore there is a high proportion of those killed
in the daily warfare as opposed to an attack. Our Canadian
plots fill up rapidly.*

LETTER FROM JOHN MCCRAE TO TOM MCCRAE,
MARCH 30, 1915

NONE OF THE MEN knew the name of the port to which
they were headed. Secrecy was impressed upon them all,
and the fear of submarine attack was ever present. Once

they entered the Bay of Biscay, they were kept from landing. Finally, after being battered about the bay for three days, it was revealed that they would disembark in the port of St. Nazaire. Rumours abounded—mostly true—that the diversion was caused by German U-boats, which were sinking any ship they encountered, whether navy, merchant, or holiday liner. All were fair game.

The brigade was received by a crowd of thousands gathered along the harbour. The well-wishers seemed mainly to be women and children, and the women were in black. It didn't take much thought to guess why. Mourning had not been so evident on Salisbury Plain, so this struck the men forcibly.

By early afternoon on February 12, 1915, the 1st Brigade CFA had disembarked in an organized and orderly fashion, unlike their experience upon landing in England. The whole division was soon on trains and heading north. As they passed through Nantes, women on porches and balconies waved handkerchiefs, but there were not enough men around to even raise a cheer.

The horses were in their own rail cars—eight to a car, with two men in each car to dispense hay and oats. For the men, the food was much to their liking: bread, bacon, bully beef, jam, tea, and sugar. They had regular stops, where there were braziers the men could cook on, latrines close to the tracks, boiled water for the men's canteens, and clean tankfuls for the horses. Both McCrae and Morrison were well pleased with these arrangements, which proved to be the norm as they went on.

On Sunday, February 14, they arrived at their first destination, detraining at Steenwerck into the flat, lush farmlands of French Flanders. As Bonfire was led off his horse car, McCrae was devastated to find that the horse had been severely kicked on his right hind leg. He had a big, infected cut, and the leg was badly swollen. McCrae rode him anyway, about four miles (six kilometres) to their first billet in the quaint village of Meteren. The sound of distant shellfire was continuous. In Meteren, they were about ten miles (sixteen kilometres) from the frontline trenches.

John McCrae, Captain Lawrence Moore Cosgrave, Colonel Dodds, and Colonel Morrison billeted in town with an elderly French widow and her daughter. The women told them graphic stories of the earlier fighting. They spoke only French, but McCrae was able to speak and understand it. Colonel Dodds also spoke considerable French, and Captain Cosgrave picked it up quickly.

The rooms the officers were in had been occupied earlier by German officers until the British drove them out.

The women took quite a shine to McCrae and his mates and nicknamed McCrae the Medicine Major. They were particularly fond of Captain Cosgrave and called him le

Bébé—the Baby—because, at twenty-five, he was young for an officer. The nickname stuck with him throughout the war.

The brigade men noted hundreds of fresh graves everywhere, little mounds of dirt with small wooden crosses. The town of Meteren was taken back from the Germans in the fall of 1914 at a terrible cost. Nearly all the buildings— homes, churches, and businesses—showed shell damage or pitting from machine guns.

McCrae had to give Bonfire a dose of vaccine. He was disappointed the horse's leg wound was so slow in healing, noting in his diary on February 9: "He seemed to know something was up when I appeared with a hypodermic syringe, and hung his head like a school boy expecting a licking. However it was not too bad after all, and he quickly cheered up."

As they travelled on horseback over the next few days, McCrae and Morrison made the rounds of batteries and met British artillerymen. The officers studied how things were being done and were given some tours and briefings by British officers.

McCrae was impressed with the "wonderful complexity" of the telephone system and the resulting excellent level of communication.

At the same time, a portion of their brigade marched to Armentières and joined with Colonel Malcolm Mercer, infantry commander of the 1st Canadian Division. They were there for observation and training only, and no guns were required.

McCrae was happy to receive a huge pile of letters from home. Among them was a letter from George Adami at McGill detailing a great disagreement going on in Montreal over the creation, location, control, and naming of a war hospital to be set up in France.

At the end of February, the 1st Brigade CFA prepared for their introduction to battle, on the British flank, about five miles from the centre of the offensive about to be launched at Neuve-Chapelle. They marched to Fleurbaix, where McCrae's brigade took over from the British 22nd Brigade Royal Field Artillery (RFA).

On March 1, the officers moved into a comfortable new billet near Fleurbaix on a farm, with Morrison in one room and McCrae, Dodds, and Cosgrave in another. McCrae noted that the horses appeared "comfy" and that Bonfire had developed a love for the local gingerbread, a particularly hard and crunchy version.

The infantry immediately suffered many casualties from bombs thrown over from the German trenches. The Canadian infantry were poorly equipped. They were not wearing helmets, only wedge caps or peaked caps. They had no proper hand grenades and sometimes improvised with jam tins filled with nails, stones, and other debris, set off with gunpowder and a fuse. They often went off prematurely, causing injury to hands and arms.

Their rifles were the long, heavy Ross rifles, an excellent sniper rifle but impractical for combat. They jammed when heated under rapid fire, and the bolt had to be bashed with a hard object, like an entrenching tool or boot heel. This was to have disastrous consequences in the coming month, once the soldiers were in Belgium.

The brigade took out a couple of snipers' houses after a request from the infantry. McCrae and Morrison went out with the 4th Battery and observed their work. McCrae watched lying on a damp haystack, while Morrison viewed the area from a small garret in the farmhouse.

Later that afternoon, McCrae set out for a meeting in a town a few miles away with the local assistant director of medical services (ADMS). On the way, he ran into the Canadian surgeon general, G. Carleton Jones. Jones as the director berated McCrae about the McGill hospital fight that Adami had mentioned in his letter, as though McCrae had any part in it. McCrae told him forcefully that he had no interest in the conflict, and, in fact, no interest in Canadian Army Medical Corps (CAMC) positions or promotions. Jones took great offence to this and tried to impress upon McCrae that, as the director was in charge of medical officers, he could do what he liked with McCrae. McCrae wrote in a letter on March 5, "I told him that I had never been gazetted to the A.M.C. and as yet was not incorporated into that holy happy band . . . I need not say that he makes me tired, as he has done for years past."

Jones seemed especially critical of the current dean of medicine at McGill, Herbert Birkett, and also resented the use of the name *McGill* for the war hospital. He intimated that it was he who had put McCrae in his current position, when it was in fact Colonel Morrison who had gotten permission from the minister of war, Sam Hughes, to take McCrae into the artillery. He was clearly furious that McCrae had chosen the artillery once more over the medical corps.

On March 10, 1915, the main concentration of British forces, five miles away from McCrae and his brigade, launched the Battle of Neuve-Chapelle with a tremendous artillery bombardment. McCrae said it was tiring on the ears, as it went on without interruption for two solid hours.

The first day's attack was successful, and the British captured a thousand German prisoners, but at the cost of heavy casualties on the British side. McCrae also heard of a German submarine being sunk, and thought the Germans were altogether "getting a good deal of their own back."

A few days later, the Germans began shelling the trenches in front of McCrae's brigade and also opened up on them with a howitzer.

Colonel Morrison went at them with all four batteries, and it turned into quite a contest. The infantry who had been shelled cheered the 1st Brigade. Major Russell Britton, commanding the 3rd Battery, asked for permission to shell two German batteries that were shelling the infantry and moving toward them in the open. McCrae noted in his war diary on March 17 that permission was granted and that Britton "put them out of business."

McCrae also wrote on March 17 that Lieutenant-General Alderson had told Morrison, "You sure stirred up a hornet's nest, as if that wasn't what we were here for."

Morrison's account of the battle was more colourful:

The windup as far as I was concerned, was that on the following day, being St. Patrick's Day, Major Britton commanding the 3rd battery, reported early in the morning that he had discovered two German batteries on our front engaged in bombarding our neighbours, and had asked leave to take them on. I gave the necessary permission, and hurried down to the battery to see the fight, which was an exceedingly pretty one. Major Britton caught the clever Boch [an Allied nickname for the Germans] with the first salvo, and the Germans reciprocated bouncing their shells off the roofs of our gun pits. One dud which was picked up showed that their range in fuse was the same as ours to a second. A lively duel ensued, and when other batteries took to hand, the Boch were soon out of business. On that part on the front there were no trenches but only parapets, which were soon breached by the guns. And as the Germans dashed past these openings they were taken on by our infantry with rifle fire, and a most enjoyable morning was had by all, especially the Infantry. The small battle lasted until noon, and was subsequently remembered as the Battle of St. Patrick's Day.

Morrison was later chastised for using so much ammunition. He received an order from the brass that had actually been written the previous day but had only got to him after the actions of March 17. They were to be rationed to three shells per gun per day. They had used over four hundred rounds in the one morning.

Morrison marched up to HQ and sarcastically asked if they should hoard ammunition while the Germans picked off their colleagues in the RFA, a question that nearly earned him a charge of insubordination. The staff let it go, but from that point on, before they moved north into Belgium, the brigade had to restrain themselves from doing what they were trained to do.

The truth was that at this time, the British were desperately short of shells, fuses, and guns. They had already requested that Canada send everything they could round up in the way of surplus guns. In France, McCrae discovered two batteries of obsolete five-inch howitzers he had commanded years before in South Africa.

A few days after the Neuve-Chapelle battle, Colonel Morrison got permission from the British staff for McCrae and himself to go out and survey the battlefield up close. This would be their first opportunity to do so in this war, and they were interested to see what the aftermath looked like. Many dead from both sides were scattered across the grounds.

A few soldiers were moving here and there in a disorganized fashion, seemingly with no purpose. Most of these were Indian soldiers. The Germans seemed to be methodically sniping them with rifles and field guns, too.

Morrison later wrote in his memoir:

> On this occasion they spotted McCrae and me as we were crossing a plowed field, and we had to lie down between the furrows for a quarter of an hour, while they endeavoured to murder us with that type of small shell then known as "pip squeaks." As we lay there we discussed the situation and came to the conclusion that we were fools to run such chances, and would only be ridiculed by our friends if anything should happen to us, and that it was not a square deal to the government that had expended so much money on our education as gunner officers, and anyhow, we would never do it again.

They eventually jumped up, ran, and got to their horses.

McCrae later reported that Bonfire gratefully acknowledged a parcel from home containing sugar and would hardly allow McCrae to unwrap it before he attacked it. He said the horse's conduct had been exemplary, although he wasn't fond of having a gun go off near his head. But McCrae noted that "he has made no fuss on any such occasion." Bonfire eventually suffered a minor shrapnel wound, and McCrae joked that they were thinking of changing his name to Gunfire.

The Battle of Neuve-Chapelle was a gradual introduction to war for Canada's artillery and infantry, most of whom were untried. The Canadian casualties were few. But for the British in the centre of the fighting, after the village was captured, they bogged down and did not advance further. About twelve thousand men on each side were killed.

On April 1, the brigade received orders to march north. A week later they were billeted around Oudezele in France, a tiny Flemish village just south of the Belgian border, about ten miles (sixteen kilometres) west of Ypres. McCrae and Morrison went for a ride to Mont Cassel, one of the few so-called mountains in the area. From there they had a fantastic view of the Ypres area. McCrae thought it was a very pretty town.

Bonfire met with another mishap when McCrae put him into a low shed for shelter from rotten weather. The horse jerked his head up at some point and hit a spike protruding from the ceiling. When McCrae found him, he had fallen and gotten up, but was wobbly on his feet. McCrae was worried he was brain-damaged, but his fears were short-lived when hay was offered a short time later and Bonfire attacked it with his usual gusto. McCrae's batman and groom, Herbert Cruickshank, said that, at first, Bonfire acted like a baby and didn't want anything, only to be petted; he realized the horse was back to normal when Bonfire bit him as usual while being groomed.

For the first couple of weeks of their stay in Oudezele, not much happened. McCrae and Morrison would inspect the batteries, which they found in excellent order, and confer with British soldiers and also with the French. They conducted standing gun drills and went on exercise rides. They inspected and re-inspected the equipment, tack, harnesses, and wagons.

Morrison wrote in his memoir that on Sunday, April 18, "We had a novelty in the shape of a sermon from Colonel John McCrae. He delivered a very thoughtful address from a pulpit consisting of an ammunition wagon."

Later that day they received orders to move again, and they marched into Belgium for the first time. They billeted in and around Poperinge, in the west of Flanders. It was a bustling crossroads of troops and supplies and of soldiers moving to and from the front. They were soon advised that a new offensive was about to begin.

Little did they suspect the enormity of what was about to take place. These mostly untried troops from Canada were about to be plunged into their first big battle of the Great War. It has been said many times that the Second Battle of Ypres was their "trial by fire," or "baptism of fire." These phrases are inadequate: there are simply no words sufficient to describe what was about to happen to these men.

6

The Second Battle of Ypres

Who amongst us on that smiling Spring day, as we held the line in front of ancient Ypres, can e'er forget that silent, menacing, all-devouring, grey-green cloud of poison gas . . . Men in their splendid strength sinking to the ground in dreadful contortions—dying after hours of agony.

EXCERPT FROM CAPTAIN LAWRENCE MOORE COSGRAVE`S BOOK, *AFTERTHOUGHTS ON ARMAGEDDON*

IN THE MIDDLE OF April 1915, the Canadian infantry came into the front line in Belgium and took possession of some vacant trenches previously held by the French in 1914. The Canadians were known as "citizen soldiers," men who had been farmers, bank tellers, teachers, loggers, and clerks before the war. These Canadians were positioned in the middle section of the Ypres Salient, salient being the term for a battlefield that "bulges" into enemy territory, leaving the troops vulnerable on three sides. The French were to their left and the British to their right.

In 1914, the French had looked upon defensive fighting with disdain. They believed in the dashing attack and the grand offensive rather than in hanging back and holding the line. As a result, the trenches the Canadian soldiers now prepared to inhabit were mostly shallow, disconnected scrapings with no parados (rear parapets) and not much of a parapet (protective wall) in front. Nor were they in a zigzag pattern, which would prevent an enemy who gained access to a trench from firing the length of it and doing maximum damage. In other words, they were utterly ineffective. The Canadians had to immediately set about making them into deep, properly fortified trenches.

These trenches had also been used as latrines, and many contained unburied or partially buried bodies. Over the years, First World War history buffs have read about arms and legs sticking out of trench walls. It was true. Major Dan Ormond of the 10th Battalion said there was a hand dangling through the parapet when they arrived, "and the men used to shake hands with it." Other stories told of men using protruding appendages as hangers for equipment. It could be that this sort of black humour helped them stem their fear of what was shaping up to be a terrific battle.

There were practical reasons for being afraid, such as the lack of proper equipment, the jamming Ross rifle, and the defective Ross bayonets, which had an unnerving habit of randomly falling off. It would be late summer before the Mills bomb—the first hand grenade issued—became available to them.

Opposite the Allied lines, a line of Germans held the high ground along the entire edge of the bulge, from north to south. The terrain looked flat, but it actually sloped upward—like the rim of a saucer—to a ridge from which the Germans could look down onto Allied lines and shoot their guns north, east, and south into Allied positions.

As days passed, the Canadian general, Arthur Currie, heard rumours from a few sources about poison gas. As early as April 13, a private named August Jager, who had given himself up to the French near Langemark, told them the Germans were going to unleash gas on them. No one believed him; in fact, they thought he was probably an enemy spy spreading false information. In any case, the use of poisonous gas went against a clause in the Hague Declaration of 1899 that prohibited any use of asphyxiating gasses as a weapon in warfare. The Allies simply refused to consider the possibility.

The fact was that the German army had some 5,370 cylinders of chlorine gas standing upright along their trenches from Langemark in the northeast to Steenstraat, at the top of the Salient. They were just waiting for favourable winds to open the valves. It seemed a reckless idea, considering that the prevailing winds were from west to east, but the days were coming when they would get their wish.

April 22 dawned "fine and cool," according to the official war diary of the 1st Brigade CFA. No breath of wind stirred. That morning, bombs were dropped from German airplanes on Poperinge, which had been, until then, far enough back of the lines to avoid being a target. The Battle of Second Ypres was beginning in earnest.

The brigade, with 2nd and 3rd Batteries—the 1st and 4th stayed behind in reserve—was ordered to move from Poperinge and march east in preparation for a major counterattack. The Germans had been battering the medieval city of Ypres (christened "Wipers" by British soldiers) with artillery for days. Now they were firing a one-ton shell every six minutes with devastating effect on the city. (The British soldiers nicknamed the shells the "Wipers Express" because the screaming sound they made reminded them of the London subway trains.) Late that afternoon, a light wind came up. It blew not from the usual prevailing direction, but came down from the northeast to the southwest.

Three-quarters of the way to Ypres, the brigade was ordered to halt and wait for further orders. As they sat on the side of the road, there was nothing to do but watch the crush of desolated civilians passing them toward the west as they fled the bombardment of their city and their homes.

To the right, they could see the towers of the magnificent Cloth Hall burning, where Ypres's cloth weaving and trading industry had once thrived. The tiny Belgian army had been smashed in the early weeks of fall 1914, the remnants escaping to Antwerp. Ypres was a purely civilian target.

As they waited, McCrae offered aid where he could. Families were passing by with all the possessions they could carry on wagons and in wheelbarrows and dogcarts. They were dirty and dishevelled, crying, many injured, all traumatized. They saw a teenager carrying his grandfather on his back. Another pushed a frail, elderly woman in a wheelbarrow. Children who were big enough to walk clung wide-eyed to their mothers' skirts or coats. Smaller ones were carried, some by siblings barely big enough to carry them.

Private Nathanial Nicholson, 16th Battalion, Canadian Scottish, wrote, "People were running hither and thither. As a matter of fact, I saw one woman carrying a baby, and the baby's head was gone, and it was quite devastating."

It's hard to imagine what was going through the young Canadians' minds as they witnessed this scene. It is certain they would have had nothing to compare it to.

At about 4:30 p.m. there was a terrific bombardment on their left. Shells were still bursting over Ypres, to their

German photograph of aftermath of the first gas attack of the First World War, Langemark, Belgium, April 23, 1915. (*Englische Schutzengraben* is translated as "English trench.") IN FLANDERS FIELDS MUSEUM, IEPER, BELGIUM

right, but now also in Vlamertinge, a small town on their left. Shortly after that, French soldiers and French colonial soldiers began to appear in the fields, coming from the north. Almost simultaneously, the 1st Brigade CFA smelled it: chlorine gas.

With the wind now sweeping down toward the west, the Germans had opened the cylinder valves, and great clouds of yellowish-green chlorine gas oozed steadily across the fields toward the Allied lines. On the road, McCrae continued to offer help where he could, but no one had a clue what to do with gas victims. Even standing over them caused one to be secondarily affected because their clothes and hair were saturated with the toxic gas.

Meanwhile, French and French North African colonial soldiers began to appear—some without rifles or caps—piled in wagons and accompanied by groups of two and three men on wagon horses with their harnesses still on. The men were alone or in groups, and some were hysterical—all were running from the north. Many Algerians, Moroccans, and Zouaves were shouting, "All is lost! All is lost!"

John McCrae wrote in his journal on April 22, 1915, "... the very picture of débacle. I must say, they were the 'tag enders' of a fighting line, rather than the line itself."

Colonel Morrison had gone ahead to reconnoitre their position by the Yser Canal. On the west bank of the canal, he surveyed the result of the gas: "... many suffering from the gas and tearing madly through the crush of fugitives with staring eyes and their faces flecked with blood and froth. Frequently these men would fall down under the feet of the mob, and roll about like mad dogs in their death agony."

Near the canal, Morrison saw two Canadian infantry battalions march over the bridge from the west, singing at the tops of their lungs, "It's a long way to Tipperary, it's a long way to go." He saw nearby artillery drivers stand up in their stirrups and shout in support.

At 3:45 a.m., the brigade received word that they were to go into position along the canal and support a counterattack in progress. Already at this hour, on the east side of the canal, the "Fighting 10th" Battalion from Calgary and Winnipeg, and the 16th Battalion, Canadian Scottish, from BC were suffering the aftermath of a battle in Kitcheners Wood. These were the two singing battalions Morrison had seen earlier.

The wood was a small oak forest a little north of Sint-Jan, in the northeast corner of Ypres. Just before midnight on April 22, the two battalions prepared to advance five hundred yards across a wide-open moonlit field in front of the wood. They were silent as they moved across the freshly plowed soil. All seemed to be going well, and they felt success was assured until—two hundred yards out—they came to a hedge with a thick strand of wire woven through it. The noise they made breaking through the wire alerted the Germans in the forest, who sent up a star shell that lit up the field as bright as day, revealing eight lines of fifteen hundred infantry soldiers marching shoulder to shoulder. The Germans then unleashed hell on the Canadians with a storm of rifle and machine-gun fire.

The men instinctively hit the deck, but they were urged to their feet by their officers. They then stormed the wood, eventually taking it in close quarters after savage hand-to-hand combat.

The two battalions fought a heroic battle and won, albeit temporarily and with terrible losses. Altogether, 259 men were killed, 406 were wounded, and 129 were missing.

Among those killed in action was the 10th Battalion commander, Lieutenant-Colonel Russell Boyle, a rancher from Crossfield, Alberta. The 10th Battalion, now the Calgary Highlanders, still wear an oak leaf on their uniform to this day in honour and remembrance of Kitcheners Wood.

Elsewhere, Canadian soldiers had held the line in spite of the poison gas and were covering much of the gap where the French had been routed. The gas was heavier than air, and many soldiers came up onto higher ground, preferring to take their chances with a bullet above rather than wallow in the gas as it sunk into the depths of their trenches. Soldiers were instructed to urinate on their handkerchiefs, as the uric acid was thought to crystalize and somewhat neutralize the chlorine.

Just before first light on April 23, McCrae and the 1st Brigade made for their designated position. They had about three miles to go and after struggling through the throngs of fleeing civilians and gassed French soldiers, arrived by 4:30 a.m. About a quarter of a mile short of the canal, McCrae put Bonfire in a farmyard in back of the lines, hopefully out of harm's way, and ran the rest of the way to the canal. The 1st Brigade had just the 2nd and 3rd Batteries with them—eight guns in all. (Lieutenant Alexis Helmer of the 2nd Battery was part of this group.)

It was here, about two miles north of Ypres along the Yser Canal, that McCrae and his fellow gunners would spend the next seventeen days.

16th Battalion, Canadian Scottish on the Yser Canal bank, with Cloth Hall of Ypres in background, April 1915. STEVE CLIFFORD, DOINGOURBIT.WORDPRESS.COM

Major John McCrae's sketch of the same position. FROM *IN FLANDERS FIELDS AND OTHER POEMS BY JOHN MCCRAE, M.D.*, 1919

On top of the canal bank were old trenches, which they initially made their working headquarters and referred to as "the Bridge." Soon Major McCrae would create his own makeshift dressing station on the west-side bank of the Yser Canal. He wrote in his war journal on Saturday, April 24, 1915,

> I got a square hole, 8 by 8, dug in the side of the hill (west), roofed over with remnants to keep out the rain, and a little sandbag parapet on the back to prevent pieces of "back-kick shells" from coming in, or prematures [exploding shells] from our own or the French guns for that matter. Some straw on the floor completed it.

Meanwhile, in the pen where McCrae had put Bonfire for safekeeping, a horse only a few yards away from him was obliterated by a direct hit from a shell, and Bonfire galloped off to safer ground.

That night, in Vlamertinge Cathedral, to the west, an improvised hospital had been created. Medics were soon overwhelmed with injuries, the severity of which they had never seen. A description by a surgeon with the 3rd Field Ambulance, Lieutenant-Colonel Watt, was included in George Adami's book, *The War Story of the C.A.M.C., 1914–1915*:

> One never-ending stream which lasted day and night for seven days without cessation: in all some five thousand two hun-

dred cases passed through our hands. Wounds here, wounds there, wounds everywhere. Legs, feet, hands missing; bleeding stumps controlled by rough field tourniquets; large portions of the abdominal walls shot away; faces horribly mutilated; bones shattered to pieces; holes that you could put your clenched fist into, filled with dirt, mud, bits of equipment and clothing, until it all became like a hideous nightmare, as if we were living the seventh hell of the damned.

McCrae's bunker looked out on the road, and the sights were horrific. He saw men and horses hit by shellfire and tried to rescue as many as he could. He watched an orderly on a bicycle get hit and travel on for eight or ten more revolutions before he fell over in a heap, dead.

A little cottage across the road served as their mess until it was hit by shells and became too dangerous most of the time. The far end of it remained intact, and they still used it during the rare quiet periods.

The German army was determined to get through Ypres to the coast, where they would take the ports, then swing around and conquer Paris. The Allies were just as determined to keep them out. The Germans continued to release gas every couple of days. McCrae reported being gassed on several occasions after the initial attack on April 22. Some came from the cylinders in the German trenches, but he also reported gas shells raining down and gassing them. He wrote on April 24, "one's eyes smarted and breathing was very laboured."

McCrae treated the wounded as best he could in his little dugout, sending them off by ambulance to rear clearing stations, from where they would eventually be transferred to war hospitals. But he often had to cross open fields back to the firing lines to treat his own men as well, a dangerous and nerve-wracking journey.

It was never quiet for more than an hour or two, and the ear-splitting din of constant artillery fire, machine guns, and rifles was hard to bear. McCrae wrote that none of their men went off their heads, but men in nearby units did, and it was not surprising.

The battle raged on, and Colonel Morrison spent much of it on the east side of the canal conferring with the infantry and determining out how best to support them with the guns. McCrae helped where he could with artillery duties, but mostly he was overwhelmed with medical challenges and could only observe the work of the guns occasionally from the Bridge.

Their food came up at dusk on supply wagons, and water was whatever they could get; they treated it with chloride of lime to kill any bacteria in it. The ammunition came on wagons, and the more intense the battle, the more wagonloads were needed. The wagons would stop behind the dyke, and the drivers would jump out and quickly carry the rounds to the gunners. McCrae wrote in his war journal on April 25, "The good old horses would swing around at the gallop, pull up in an instant, and stand puffing and blowing, but with their heads up, as if to say, "Wasn't that well done?" It makes you want to kiss their dear old noses, and assure them of a peaceful pasture once more."

Later that day, there was tremendous shelling. Three farms in front of them on the east side of the canal were shelled and burned down one after another. The brigade's telephone-wagon team was hit, and McCrae managed to save one horse, but two others died. After dark, shelling became even heavier and went on until the early hours. McCrae reckoned there were probably two hundred rounds, singly or in pairs. Each one that burst would light up McCrae's dugout, and clods of dirt and debris would rain down on them.

Colonel Morrison was somewhere outside in the on-slaught, looking for safe haven. He tried the mess house, but it was too heavily shelled. Eventually, four men spent an anxious night in the dark of McCrae's tiny eight-by-eight-foot hole: McCrae, Cosgrave, Morrison, and his adjutant.

Another gas attack came on April 29, but the wind shifted back to its normal path, from west to east, and they were spared. McCrae was amazed at how—throughout all this—the birds, particularly the larks, continued to sing sweetly, as though all was as usual.

The entire eight-mile front of the Salient was engaged with heavy artillery fire coming in and going out. There were no quiet spots. At one point the Canadians were firing their own guns back to back at German positions at the north and south ends of the Salient.

On May 2, intense, heavy shelling went on all night, increasing toward morning. Finally there came a lull. Lieutenant Helmer was talking to Lieutenant Owen Hague at the guns when he suffered a direct shell hit. Helmer was obliterated. Hague was badly wounded in the thighs and sent out by ambulance.

McCrae ordered all the remains of Alexis Helmer's body gathered up and put into two army blankets. These were pinned together into a semblance of a human shape, and Lieutenant Helmer was buried. Major McCrae said the burial-service prayers over him as well as he could remember them. He noted that there were no chaplains anywhere near the hot zone and commented that perhaps CF (Chaplain to the Forces) actually meant Cold Feet.

While the official war diary states bluntly, "May 2/15 Canal Bank, Ypres Lt. Helmer killed & Lt. Hague severely wounded while observing," McCrae's own diary of May 2, 1915, records the event thus:

> Lieut H_____ was killed at the guns. He was (our mess sec'y and) a very nice boy—grad of RMC & McGill. His diary's last words were, "It has quieted a little and I shall try and get a good sleep!" His girl's picture had a hole right through it and we buried it with him. I said the committal service over him, as well as I could from memory. A soldier's death!

In Flanders Fields

—

In Flanders fields the poppies blow
Between the crosses, row on row,
That mark our place; and in the sky
The larks, still bravely singing, fly
Scarce heard amid the guns below.

We are the Dead. Short days ago
We lived, felt dawn, saw sunset glow,
Loved, and were loved, and now we lie
    In Flanders fields.

Take up our quarrel with the foe:
To you from failing hands we throw
The torch; be yours to hold it high.
If ye break faith with us who die
We shall not sleep, though poppies grow
    In Flanders fields

Punch
Dec 8·1915

John McCrae

"In Flanders Fields," in John McCrae's hand. INFLANDERSFIELDS.CA

Lieutenant Helmer was the sixth man killed that day in the 1st Brigade CFA, and there were fifty casualties. Some of their guns were also hit and destroyed. They were down to twelve guns, from sixteen. Owen Hague was transported out to a field hospital in Hazebrouck, but died that evening of his wounds.

April became unseasonably warm, and soon poppies sprang out of the ground in the churned-up earth and other places where soil was disturbed. In their expanding make-shift cemetery, poppies had grown throughout.

In Morrison's memoir, he only refers to the French cemetery nearby at this time. In a German aerial photograph of the 1st Brigade's position, a small cemetery with about thirty-five fresh graves can be seen just before the bend in the Yser Canal, which was the north end of the brigade's position. Where they buried Alexis Helmer is not known. It is likely that many or all of those buried along the canal during the Second Battle of Ypres were later blown out of the ground by the fighting. Some may have been reburied, but many were lost forever. Lieutenant A.H. Helmer's name is on the Menin Gate in Ypres, along with the names of more than fifty-four thousand officers and men whose final resting places remain unknown.

Shortly after Helmer's death, McCrae was sitting on the back step of an ambulance, looking upon the red flowers as they nodded in the breeze, when the first immortal lines of his poem popped into his head: "In Flanders Fields the poppies grow between the crosses row on row, that mark our place." ("Grow" was later changed to "blow.")

He makes no mention of conceiving the poem in his letters or diary at the time.

It is hard to know definitively the evolution of the poem following that first inspiration. It was said that Colonel Morrison rescued the poem after he found it discarded as a crumpled piece of paper on the ground near the canal. Another account said that Captain Francis Scrimger, VC, a surgeon with the 14th Royal Montreal Regiment and a McGill colleague of McCrae's, happened by, picked it up, and saved it.

One thing is certain: it took McCrae a long time to fully take ownership of the poem, which was probably a spontaneous outpouring of grief for Alexis Helmer and the other young men destroyed in the Second Battle of Ypres.

In the following days, the intensive shelling continued, and a huge force of German soldiers began massing for an attack. McCrae mentions that "the accursed Ger. aeroplanes" were over them again, pinpointing their positions and generally causing anxiety. They fired at them from the ground, but with no success.

The battle increased in ferocity. On May 7, they were heavily shelled, and by May 8, the 1st Brigade CFA were down to only seven guns. McCrae wrote in his war diary on May 8, "Of these, two were smoking at every joint, and the levers were so hot, that the gunners used sacking for their hands."

The war diary of 1st Brigade CFA notes on the same day, May 8, 1915, "Firing so heavy oil in buffers boiling. Springs broken or tired. Packing burnt out."

They began to hear disconcerting rumours of retirement (retreat), but nothing was certain, only that they had to keep firing their guns for as long as they worked and there were men fit to fire them. McCrae wrote in his diary on May 8, "That sort of night brings a man down to his bare skin, I promise you." It was clearly a harrowing night, with the potential for death at any moment, the uncertainty, and the relentless earsplitting noise.

The rumours turned out to be true. The next day, May 9, they were ordered to get ready to move. As McCrae sat in his dugout preparing for the final order to move out, a little black-and-white dog jumped into his bunker and proceeded to dig furiously in the hard dirt in one corner. She only managed a shallow hole about two inches deep, and then sat in it, shaking from head to foot. McCrae wrote, "She sat down and shook, looking most plaintively at me. A few minutes later her owner came along, a French soldier. Bissac was her name, but she would not leave me at the time."

After firing some thirty-six hundred rounds at the enemy that day, the 1st Brigade CFA finally got the order to move out at dusk. They had to get their guns out by hand; using the horse teams would have taken too much time and made them too vulnerable to enemy shellfire. They marched all night, all the way back to Steenwerck, in northern France, where they had first detrained back in February. On their way they were shocked and angered when passing soldiers told them of the sinking of the passenger ship *Lusitania* by a German U-boat. They were also congratulated for "good shooting" in the battle they had just fought in.

McCrae wrote of his pleasure in reuniting with his horse: "I was glad to get on dear old Bonfire again. We made about sixteen miles and got to our billets at dawn."

He noted that the horses had suffered heavily, too, and that Bonfire had another, small shrapnel wound: "It is healing, and the dear old fellow is very fit."

McCrae was annoyed that after all their travails by the canal, the Canadian newspapers erroneously reported that their batteries were in reserve. The truth was that, despite being vastly outmanned and outgunned, the mostly green Canadians were able to stop the Germans from getting through Ypres.

They had lost half their men in the firing line and been in the most savage of battles. For seventeen days they had not changed clothes or had a proper wash. In the entire time, while McCrae was awake, shellfire and gunfire continued non-stop, never ceasing for more than sixty seconds. His overall impression was of having lived through a night-

16th Battalion Canadian Scottish survivors of the Battle of
Kitcheners Wood, April 26, 1915. STEVE CLIFFORD, DOINGOURBIT.
WORDPRESS.COM

mare: "My clothes, kit, boots, and dugout at various times
were sadly bloody."

The Canadians settled briefly into billets near
Steenwerck and set about repairing their battered guns.
On May 12, General Edwin Alderson, the British general
still commanding the 1st Canadian Division, came by to
congratulate them for their part in Ypres. He read con-
gratulatory messages from King George V, Robert Borden,
(Canada's prime minister), the Canadian Governor General
Sir John French, and General Sir Horace Smith-Dorrien.

McCrae's impression was that Alderson really had no idea what they'd been doing at all—neither he nor any of his staff was seen near the canal once during the whole battle. McCrae was less than impressed and noted, "I think it may be said that we saw the whole show from the soup to the coffee."

That was certainly true of the Second Battle of Ypres. The men were numb. They were filthy. They were spent, and in dire need of rest. But it was not to be.

7

Festubert

For man was forced to think, and learn to know himself, to an-
alyze his deepest thoughts, and sometimes, perhaps, in those
solemn moments when one hovers between life and death, a
few of us may have seen beyond the veil, where all things are
known; and so—our vivid, horrified hate of the enemy, roused
in the bloody salient of Ypres and kept fresh by Festubert and
Givenchy, slowly changed, as we sat through the long, weary
winter days, to perhaps another, perhaps, deeper feeling.

EXCERPT FROM CAPTAIN LAWRENCE MOORE COS-
GRAVE'S BOOK, *AFTERTHOUGHTS ON ARMAGEDDON*

IN MID-MAY, with only five days having passed since their
hellish ordeal at the Yser Canal, the brigade received word

that they were to provide support to a huge British offensive under way near Festubert, in the Artois region of France.

A new kind of nightmare unfolded. They began digging their batteries into various positions on April 14 near Le Bizet. They repaired and restored their guns, and found they were almost back to full strength, minus one gun from the 1st Battery. They billeted around Steenwerck for a few days before receiving orders to march to La Bassée.

A note in the brigade's war diary notes, "March very trying." This is significant. Regimental war diaries are matter-of-fact records of the daily activities of brigades and regiments. They rarely contain emotion, opinion, or speculation. Even the deaths of their men are written up in a terse manner limited to basic facts such as the deceased person's name, the date and location of death, and—sometimes—what the deceased was doing at the time of death.

Despite the "trying" march cited in the brigade's diary, the battered and exhausted men had no option but to carry on, marching through the pitch-dark night and the pouring rain, over damaged roads littered with shattered wagons and the bodies of the dead, toward La Bassée. They had to rely on their horses, as they could see nothing.

A short distance away from their destination, an officer from staff HQ appeared and ordered the men to return to their previous billets. The next day, they were sent to another exposed and dangerous position northwest of La

Bassée. What ensued was a nightmare of confusing, conflicting orders. At times, they had no clue whose command they were under.

For John McCrae, who abhorred inefficiency, this would have been hard to tolerate, all the more so because they were helpless to understand anything in the chaos.

The next night they were again ordered to march, only to be stopped on the road by a staff officer who knew nothing except that they had to wait. Eventually they were told they were to billet at a particular farm, whose owners had not been informed. The farmers put up a fight but were eventually overruled. Probably the depleted, exasperated 1st Brigade felt they had no choice but to assert themselves.

The overwhelming stench of hundreds of dead, unburied British and German soldiers hung over the whole area. Nearly all the dead lay where they fell, in trenches, shell holes, by roadsides, and in open fields. McCrae treated the wounded as he was called to. Many men were left for long periods because it was too dangerous to retrieve them. This led to many more deaths than might otherwise have occurred had the wounded been attended to sooner.

Most of the brigade's shooting efforts were rewarded with savage retaliation. On May 27, McCrae wrote that the German guns "gave us a blacksmithing and drew a perfect hornet's nest about our heads."

On one occasion, the brigade's gunners were ordered under cover as German heavy guns smashed their emplacements and limbers and exploded some of their ammunition, damaging a gun and destroying the telephone lines.

A couple of days later, McCrae saw old front trenches and support trenches from an earlier front line. All were full of unburied or partially buried bodies. The smell was staggering. The ground was strewn with parts of uniforms, broken equipment, pouches, and shattered rifles. The trenches were muddy and waterlogged, and the blackened faces of the dead, with flies buzzing loudly over them, were everywhere. McCrae wrote in his war journal on May 29, "The whole ground is seamed in all directions by trenches, and scattered defences, wire, sand-bags and dugouts in bewildering disorder."

On May 30, the order came that McCrae was to leave the artillery and report to Shorncliffe, in England. He was finally to be pressed into service with the Canadian Army Medical Corps. His replacement on the front had not arrived yet, so he would have to wait. He took a walk later that day and surveyed the damage in the area. All farms and buildings were destroyed by shell fire. The steel girders of a ruined stone building stuck out and were twisted in all directions.

Though he had escaped injury in the latest turmoil, McCrae did not elude one common pestilence of trench warfare. He wrote on May 31, "On a personal note, I grieve to find out I have got lice as a result of a week without getting one's clothes off, and sleeping in trenches and on doubtful straw."

He spent his last couple of days organizing his kit, saying goodbye to the men and to his dear friends Colonel Morrison, Captain Cosgrave, and Colonel Dodds. He wrote that friendships forged in such circumstances are "apt to be the real thing," and he was sorry to leave them in such a hot corner.

On June 2, McCrae left the battle zone to make his way to London. He left Bonfire with his groom, Cruickshank, for the time being. He wrote in his journal that day:

Rode thru Bethune . . . to Chocques, where I said goodbye to Bonfire for the present. As soon as the hospital is in France, I shall send, and they will despatch Bonfire with the requisite passes & money to march to the sea; a couple of days will suffice; I hope nothing happens to him in the meantime. Cruickshank's deep affection for him is a great safeguard.

Or so he thought.

War Hospital

Col McCrae [with his departure from the artillery, McCrae was promoted from major to lieutenant-colonel] was a real soldier, but sometimes I think he carried it too far, for he would have a cold water bath every morning, and sometimes I had to break the ice for him to get it, shave in cold water, and always seemed to refuse any comfort I may have been able to obtain.

EXCERPT FROM AN UNDATED LETTER WRITTEN AFTER
THE WAR, FROM PRIVATE WILLIAM DODGE (MCCRAE'S
CAMC BATMAN) TO A MRS. MATTHEWS

MCCRAE MADE HIS WAY to London by train from Chocques, and then by ship from Boulogne. He soon made contact

No. 3 tent hospital at Dannes-Camiers, France, Autumn 1915
GUELPH MUSEUMS

with the McGill men there and was happy to catch up with his friends George Adami and John Todd (who had given Bonfire to him), among others. They were in the final planning stages of a new war hospital to be called No. 3 Canadian General Hospital (McGill).

McCrae wrote in his war diary on June 3, "Saw General Jones. I now become Lt. Col. in the Can. Army Med. Corps. Here I'm afraid my diary drops to banality."

It's not hard to imagine what McCrae was thinking and feeling with that blunt entry. His old nemesis, Surgeon General Guy Carleton Jones, had finally won. It is also well known that when an individual soldier is taken out of battle and leaves his close comrades behind in danger, he often suffers severe guilt. Unless severely wounded, he will usually return to them as soon as possible.

In London, McCrae lunched at the home of Sir William and Lady Grace Osler; Eddie Archibald and Harvey Cushing, who had been serving with a Harvard unit in the American Ambulance in France, were there as well. Cushing and McCrae had worked together at Johns Hopkins under Sir Osler in 1899.

On June 9, Grace Osler wrote of McCrae in a letter to her sister (quoted in Harvey Cushing's *The Life of Sir William Osler*):

Sunday afternoon Jack McCrae came—I'm glad and sorry you did not hear him. He looked thin and worn, but was intensely interesting; 31 days in the trenches with 8 days' rest . . . His clothes were awful. I have sent everything to the cleaner's. He says the British hatred for the Germans increases daily since the Lusitania . . . He feels the Allies will win but nothing can be ended except by absolute exhaustion. The nerve strain [associated with shell shock] he says is beyond any sensation possible to describe. They were at it day and night, saving the situation as we know. Really, I felt sick when he left Monday night. Jack lay in the garden all (Monday).

The preparations continued, and in July 1915 the first incarnation of No. 3 Canadian General Hospital was set up near Etaples in northwestern France, between the small villages of Camiers, to the south, and Dannes, to the north. The McGill staff arrived, including McCrae and most of his McGill colleagues. Included on the staff was a young man slated to be the quartermaster, Edward "Revere" Osler, the son and only child of Sir William and Grace Osler. McCrae had known Revere since he was a toddler, when he was at Johns Hopkins in Baltimore.

Durbar tents were sent as a gift from Indian royalty: large marquis tents for the patients and bell tents for the staff. They would accommodate 1,050 patients. The tent hospital was but a stone's throw from the English Channel, just barely inside the dunes. This proximity to the sea would become a factor once winter set in.

The last week before the hospital was scheduled to open, John McCrae, Eddie Archibald, and Donald Hingston set off for Paris. The three doctors planned to visit several war hospitals in the area to study their medical and surgical work and inspect how they managed their heating, electricity, and sewage systems.

They visited the American Ambulance Hospital in Neuilly, where Major Harvey Cushing had been that spring. McCrae and his companions had heard reports of Cushing's surgical excellence. Cushing eventually became renowned as a neurosurgeon pioneer who learned much of his trade from removing bullets and shrapnel from the brains of First World War soldiers.

One of the nurses working at the hospital in Neuilly had known McCrae before the war but didn't recognize him at first. She thought he had aged fifteen years.

McCrae was told that Bonfire would not be returned to him. It seems the CAMC brass had decided to take away the horses of the medical staff. It also seems certain that Surgeon General Jones had had a hand in it. McCrae made a personal plea by letter, explaining that he and Bonfire had been through too much together and it would be wrong to separate them. His letter made its way up the chain of command. In a letter to Marjorie Todd, who, with her husband, John, had given Bonfire to McCrae, McCrae wrote that eventually the inspector general of communications had arranged for the horse to be returned to him.

Some speculated that Minister Sam Hughes played a part in getting Bonfire returned to McCrae. Whatever the case, McCrae was relieved and delighted to welcome Bonfire on July 16, 1915, when he arrived at Dannes-Camiers after travelling by train with his groom, Herbert Cruickshank.

On August 8, 1915, No. 3 Canadian General Hospital (McGill) opened for business. After rigorous training rehearsals, the staff braced themselves for the convoys of sick and wounded that were soon to come. They were to treat them for three weeks and either get them well or send them on to England for further care. Meanwhile, a terrible new weapon had come into use, the flame-thrower.

Officers of No. 3 Canadian General Hospital (McGill), Boulogne, November 1916. GUELPH MUSEUMS

No. 3 Hospital saw some of the first casualties of that brutal device.

Distinguished visitors began to appear, including Minister of War Sam Hughes, Sir Max Aitken (Lord Beaverbrook), and George Adami, among others. McCrae was not a fan of these visits, nor of anything he perceived to be a waste of his time or disruptive to his work. An exception, though, was the visit from his well-loved mentor and friend, William Osler, who turned up on September 7. Osler wrote a diary of the trip to a friend. This excerpt from

Osler's diary is quoted in Harvey Cushing's *The Life of Sir William Osler*: "You would be amused to peek through the fly of a tent and see me sitting up on a camp bed with a pad on my knee! Such a comfortable billet! I have not slept in a tent for forty years."

Shortly after Sir William's arrival, McCrae took him on a tour of the battle zone, including several of the places he had been with the Canadian Field Artillery. Sir William was in awe of the intensive battlefield activity—the lines of artillery on the move; the men on foot and on horseback; the not-too-distant shellfire; and the "aeroplanes," observation balloons, and endless convoys of supply trucks and wagons.

In an excerpt from Michael Bliss's book, *William Osler: A Life in Medicine*, a letter by Osler is quoted thus: "Col McCrae has been fighting all thro the district and took us to several spots on which his battery was stationed. Everywhere great squares of graves—marked with the names of the men of the Regiments."

In a letter home that August, McCrae said he expected to wish often that he had stuck by the artillery. Colonel Morrison had offered him a brigade major's job, and if it was his own decision to make, he would have taken it. His decision to stay with the hospital may, among other factors, have been influenced by his concern for his parents, particularly his mother. Also, he had heard an ongoing rumour that Bonfire would be taken away again and noted, "That would be the last straw." Finally, a sympathetic general assured him he would be able to keep his charger. McCrae wrote of his Scottish groom, "Cruickshank's ears suffered from the width of his grin at the news."

The first major test of No. 3 came with a big wave of wounded from the Battle of Loos. On September 22, 1915, the hospital received orders to evacuate all patients who could be moved and make room for casualties expected from a new offensive. They were told this was a "crisis expansion" and that five hundred extra beds must be provided. Two hundred and ninety patients were evacuated to England within three days.

Four days later, on September 26, the first wounded arrived at No. 3, and soon all doctors and nursing sisters were operating at their utmost. The first soldiers were from the Gordon Highlanders, who had been badly hit. Some were already dead, and others were dying. For several consecutive days, the operating room staff performed about thirty surgeries per day. Over one thousand patients were admitted that first week.

A private wrote in his diary (excerpted from *No. 3 Canadian Canadian General Hospital (McGill)*), "This week—the busiest since we opened—is a confusion to me of blood, gaping wounds, saline, and bichloride. Few particular events remain clearly in my mind."

The hospital staff celebrated what early arrivals from Loos believed was a success, but their celebrations were dashed when later scores of wounded informed them that the Loos attack was a failure.

There were a few notable things about the Battle of Loos. It was Britain's biggest offensive of 1915, and it marked the country's first use of poison gas against the Germans, much of which blew back and poisoned their own soldiers. On a more personal note, something happened that was especially tragic to many, including John McCrae: the disappearance of Rudyard Kipling's son Jack, who was reported missing in action by the Irish Guards.

Lieutenant Jack Kipling was found to have been killed in the Battle of Loos on September 27, 1915, barely six weeks after his eighteenth birthday. It became well known after his death that Kipling was clinically blind and that all kinds of strings had been pulled, following his rejection by the Navy on account of it, to get him into the infantry. One can hardly imagine the grief and probable remorse experienced by his father, who had played a major part in getting him into the army.

The tent hospital at Dannes-Camiers served many wounded, and was undoubtedly a great training ground, but its limitations became apparent during the first winter gale that blew in from the English Channel. October 25 was marked by a storm that staff at No. 3 would never forget. Tents were blown down and re-erected again and again. Wards were completely flooded, and nursing sisters worked sometimes knee-deep in mud. Wounded and sick soldiers suffered from the wind and damp, and it became an ordeal for the nursing sisters, too, as they tried, often vainly, to keep their patients warm and comfortable. For McCrae, it brought back memories of Salisbury Plain.

McCrae's landlord and friend from McGill, surgeon Edward "Eddie" Archibald, also working at No. 3, saw clear evidence in Dannes-Camiers that John McCrae was suffering from war trauma.

In a letter to his wife in the fall of 1915, Archibald wrote that Jack's nerves "were clearly knocked endways." Suffering classic symptoms of what is now called post-traumatic stress disorder (PTSD), McCrae was irritable, at times isolated himself, had trouble concentrating, and was argumentative. He needed more rest than usual and was definitely not the man his friends and colleagues had known in Montreal.

Although the officers had huts, McCrae insisted on sleeping in a bell tent. It was as if he didn't want to be in more comfortable quarters than the soldiers in the field. He still wore his artillery uniform, with the gunner's badge on his cap.

He continued to tinker with his poem "In Flanders Fields," and that fall, at the urging of Colonel Birkett who was familiar with McCrae's writing from *The McGill University Magazine*, McCrae sent it to the British magazine *The Spectator*. It was rejected, and McCrae commented, "The babe hath returned unto its mother's arms."

Captain Francis Scrimger, VC, another McGill doctor, convinced McCrae to try the magazine *Punch*, which published the poem on December 8, 1915 strangely, however, without the author's name. The editor made some minor changes, including changing word *grow* in the second line to *blow*, which stuck and is how we know the poem today.

Starting with Loos, McCrae and his pathology department had to deal with terrible infections of a variety and severity they'd never seen before. Sir Andrew Macphail, who commanded the 6th Canadian Field Ambulance, explains the provenance of these infections contracted from the Flemish battlefields in this quote from R.C. Fetherstonagh's book, *No. 3 Canadian General Hospital (McGill) 1914–1919*:

> The surgeon has no unfair advantage. From his point of view never was a filthier war waged. From time immemorial Flanders has been the battlefield of Europe, and in the intervals of peace the land was most carefully farmed. The inhabitants gather up all the excreta, their own included, and use it to fertilize that land, with the result that the soil is deeply infected.

The heavily manured fields also led to a new and awful phenomenon known as gas gangrene, a bacterial infection which led to gas forming in the tissues; it was a fast-spreading, life-threatening emergency.

Colonel John Elder, officer in charge of surgery, stated,

> We have now done over 500 operations and admitted more than 3000 patients. We have had many secondary haemorrhages, due, I fancy, to the disintegrating character of the organisms infecting the wounds. Some of the smells of the wounds are awful, and the necessary incisions are ghastly.

Colonel Herbert Birkett, the commanding officer of No. 3, added: "I have seen cases in the Operating Room in which the tissues are so rotten with infection that portions of muscle tissue can be removed by the handful."

McCrae is not mentioned much in the official hospital history of No. 3 at Dannes-Camiers. He was likely still suffering the aftermath of the Second Battle of Ypres and Festubert.

After the fall and winter storms made it clear they had to find a new site for the hospital, Birkett, Elder, and McCrae travelled north to Boulogne on November 21 to inspect a Jesuit school on the Calais Road outside of Boulogne. It was, at that time, occupied by the Meerut (Indian) Stationary Hospital. They agreed that with some major alterations, it would make a suitable new home for No. 3 Canadian General Hospital (McGill).

While the old hospital was dismantled and the new site was being set up, most of the staff were dispersed temporarily to help out at surrounding hospitals. McCrae referred to "nervous cases" he'd seen at Dannes-Camiers and commented that "many patients arrived from the front bankrupt as to their nervous systems." There was no term at that time to describe what was later called "shell shock." Sufferers often had elevated heart rates, as high as 150 beats per minute. In many cases, the soldier had not been exposed to shellfire, but may have been at the front for prolonged lengths of time and seen heavy combat. There were other cases, though, where exposure to the fighting had been brief but violent. It could still result in "exhausted nerves," as they referred to it then.

The book *No. 3 Canadian General Hospital (McGill) 1914–1919* alludes to yet another story about the origins of the poem "In Flanders Fields." At the end of the last chapter, before the hospital move from Dannes-Camiers to Boulogne, it tells of a morning in November in which McCrae shows the CO of the hospital, Colonel Birkett, a few pencilled lines of a poem written on a torn piece of wrapping paper.

Another interesting detail about the poem appears in the diary of a nursing sister at No. 3, Claire Gass, dated October 30, 1915. It is a copy of "In Flanders Fields" she had written out before it is published and before it was said to have been shown to Birkett by McCrae.

* * *

No. 3 Hospital moved north and settled onto twenty-five acres under the watchful eye of Emperor Napoleon atop the Colonne de la Grande Armée monument on the edge of the city of Boulogne. On January 28, 1916, the hospital resumed operations in its new location.

In March, pathologist Captain Lawrence Rhea, who worked directly under McCrae, presented a report to hospital CO Colonel Birkett about fifteen post-mortems he had conducted on soldiers who had died from brain injury. Only one had died from a fragment of a shell that had lodged in his brain. The rest died from skull fragments that had penetrated their brains, but the projectile itself had only glanced off the skull without penetrating it. The recommendation was that steel helmets would save many lives. It seems so obvious now, but the Canadian soldiers did not wear helmets until 1916!

Lieutenant-Colonel John McCrae continued to treat soldiers, and as the officer in charge of medicine—the top pathologist—it was his job to diagnose disease, formulate treatments, dispense medicines, and supervise laboratory work.

In 1916, the two battles the Canadians were involved in created a continuous deluge of casualties. One began June 2 at Hill 60 in the southern Ypres Salient area of Belgium, and the other, the massive Battle of the Somme, launched on July 1 on flat, French farmland. From the Somme alone, between July 1 and July 15, No. 3 took in over 4,600 patients.

McCrae's devotion to the soldiers was unstinting, but he continued to withdraw outside of his medical duties. He developed a more severe military bearing and became impatient with anyone who did not show the same dedication. If someone dared called him "Doctor" instead of "Colonel," they'd get a blast.

His saving grace was Bonfire; McCrae would take long solitary rides on the horse after work at the hospital. One of his favourite haunts was the Vallée du Denacre, right across the road from Napoleon on his pillar. It was a secluded wood, full of songbirds, and featured a lovely stream and a path lined with blackberry bushes. There was also an estaminet (a type of pub–restaurant), Estaminet 2e Moulin, beside the stream, where he would tether Bonfire and watch the water flow over the water wheel there.

Soon there was a new addition to his animal friends in the form of a sweet French spaniel named Bonneau. Bonneau belonged to the hospital caretakers, the Debakker family, but upon meeting McCrae, the dog abandoned his owners and moved into McCrae's bell tent with him. As at Dannes-Camiers, McCrae would not lodge in the nicer officers' quarters. In a detailed aerial diagram of the 26-acre hospital grounds, there is a lone bell tent beside the pathology laboratory. It is almost certainly Colonel McCrae's quarters.

Andrew Macphail, McCrae's friend and the editor of *The McGill University Magazine*, spoke of McCrae thus:

John McCrae, Bonfire, Herbert Cruickshank, and Bonneau at No. 3, Boulogne, 1917. GUELPH MUSEUMS

"To walk in the streets with him was a slow procession. Every dog and every child one met must be spoken to and each made to answer." He may have isolated himself from his adult colleagues, but his love for animals, and children, when he came across them, never wavered.

McCrae was a prolific letter writer, diarist, and journal writer throughout his life, and this is fortunate for us in helping to understand him. He wrote letters and postcards home to his nieces and nephews. To his sister Geills's four children, he signed his letters as Bonfire or Bonneau and included a respective hoof or paw print. The children were no doubt delighted to receive them. Here is a letter from Bonfire to "Serg.-Major Jack Kilgour" (who was about six at this time).

From Bonfire to Serg.-Major Jack Kilgour
     August 6th, 1916

Did you ever have a sore hock? I have one now, and Cruick-shank puts bandages on my leg. He also washed my white socks for me. I'm glad you got my picture. My master is well, and the girls tell me I am looking well, too. The ones I like best give me biscuits and sugar, and sometime flowers. One of them did not want to give me some mignonette the other day because she said it would make me sick. Another one sends me bags of carrots. If you don't know how to eat carrots, tops and all, you had better learn, but I suppose you are just a boy, and do not know how good oats are.

The letter was signed "Bonfire, His Mark," with a tiny drawing of a horse shoe.

In a letter to Marjorie Todd in January 1916, he wrote, referring to Bonfire:

His coat is a little thick and wintry but he looks very well. And popular! Some of the sisters [nursing sisters] carry sugar on the chance of meeting him, and the rogue has learned to kiss, his groom being the preceptor (no, not I!!) He puts his lips up to one's cheek, and wags his under lip in the funniest fashion. And no respecter of persons! I found him kissing a little French girl the other day. A few days ago, too, I came out and found him standing quietly with his head down: I found on getting closer that he had his groom's coat-skirt in his teeth. I think it is his way of taking his nursemaid's hand, but I don't know, being only human and therefore handi-capped in my understanding.

Bonfire was a great favourite of the local French children, and also of the nursing sisters, causing McCrae to remark that "they love the horse more than they love me." In a letter to his mother, he said he wished his young nephew Jack could see Bonfire "getting his face brushed; he shuts his eyes tight, like a small boy, and when he gets his nose washed there is much puffing and blowing as two small boys would make."

The asthma McCrae had suffered from for most of his life was exacerbated from his being gassed several times during the Second Battle of Ypres. With the cold, damp climate of coastal northwestern France, he suffered persistent lung problems while working at the hospital, including repeated bouts of bronchitis, pleurisy, colds, and coughs. In a photograph of officers of the hospital taken in the ruins of the Jesuit school during November 1916, McCrae's cap is askew; he still has a gunner's badge on his cap, and what appears to be a sidearm. He's also wearing shoes, rather than his usual leather riding boots. His service record indicates that he was sick with pleurisy for most of November and had been hospitalized near the time the photograph was taken. His gaze seems indicative of the unfocused "thousand-yard stare," the particular glassy and distant gaze now associated with PTSD.

* * *

In total, No. 3 Hospital admitted 36,141 patients during 1916. One hundred and fifty-one patients died, which, given the huge number admitted, doesn't seem too bad. Hundreds of patients that year were victims of the various phases of the Battle of the Somme, which began July 1 and dragged on until mid-November.

The hospital statistics are impressive, but we must not forget the thousands who never made it to a hospital. They died on the battlefield. The first day of the Somme alone accounted for some 29,000 British deaths.

The year 1917 dawned with brutally cold weather. McCrae wrote in his diary, excerpted in *No. 3 Canadian General Hospital (McGill) 1914–1919*:

> The cruel cold is still holding. Everyone is suffering, and the men in bed in the wards cannot keep warm. For my own part, I do not think I have ever been more uncomfortable. Everything is so cold that it hurts to pick it up. To go to bed is a nightmare, and to get up a worse one.

It helps put this description into perspective to recall that McCrae grew up in southwestern Ontario, where winters can be very cold and snowy.

On April 9, 1917, the four divisions of Canadians under Lieutenant-General Sir Julian Byng and Canadian Corps Commander Arthur Currie launched the Battle of Vimy Ridge, which was a masterpiece of planning, preparation, and tactical genius. Four days later, supported by British and other Allied units, the ridge and all its German

John McCrae and Bonneau, Boulogne 1917. GUELPH MUSEUMS

trenches and fortifications were firmly in Canadian hands. It was said by some to be the birth of Canada "unto a nation of its own."

The night of April 10, the wounded began to arrive at No. 3 in a wave of convoys, and the number steadily increased. By the morning of April 11, the operating theatre was in action for fourteen solid hours. Many terrible wounds were from machine-gun fire.

Major-General Edward Morrison was in command of all the Canadian artillery, as he had been since 1916. Although Vimy Ridge was only 70 miles (113 kilometres) from No. 3 on the Calais Road, it was a world away. On April 11, Morrison wrote McCrae that "it certainly was the greatest day in the history of the gunners . . . If you were only here, I think my enjoyment would be complete." Then Morrison added a colourful anecdote about Byng, who was very fond of the Canadians and got a kick out of their peculiar expressions:

> You know General Byng delights in Canadian slang. He repeats it over and chuckles to himself when it is expressive. He likes my expression, "Go to it." At the height of the battle when I got the report that we had taken the Ridge, I went to him and said, "General, everything is jake! [*Jake* was slang at the time for A-OK]. We are shelling the retiring Bosches." He sprung his jolly smile and gave the historic order, "Morrison, go to it"! (This is history "as she is made," not as she is writ!)

Morrison added a PS to the letter, asking McCrae to write out a copy of "In Flanders Fields," for General Byng.

Learning of the victory at Vimy, and receiving this effusive personal account from his dear friend Morrison, would have provided a rare bright spot in McCrae's otherwise bleak days of treating the many casualties of the fighting.

In spring 1917, McCrae had the well-known photograph taken of himself with Bonneau, the spaniel. He said it required patience, but eventually he got the dog sit up on his haunches and place his paws over McCrae's outstretched arm. With typical humility, he said in a letter to his mother, in which the photo was enclosed, "You must admit it is one of the best dog pictures you ever saw. I'm only an accident in the picture."

Bonneau was as well loved as Bonfire and delighted the soldiers in the wards when he would do rounds with McCrae. He would occasionally carry a stick the whole way, and once he came along with a large bone. Bonneau had a serious, even sorrowful look, but it didn't stop him from being friendly and playful. McCrae referred to his manner as "grave."

In the middle of 1917, Revere Osler (Sir William's son) had gotten bored of being a quartermaster at No. 3 Hospital. He tried to get into a field ambulance unit, but that effort became mired in red tape. He then decided to become a combatant and join the Royal Artillery. Sir William Osler wrote at the time, "Long association with Jack McCrae has made him a bit bloodthirsty."

It's possible that McCrae may have had some influence over the younger Osler. McCrae had known Revere since he was a child in Baltimore. One imagines McCrae might have regaled him over the years with swashbuckling tales of the Boer War and other adventurous stories of the Empire. Also, McCrae made no secret, especially early on in the war, of his hostility toward the Germans and his resolve that they must be beaten whatever the cost.

Whatever the reason, by way of determined string pulling, Edward Revere Osler finally got himself out of the Canadian Army Medical Corps and accepted into the Royal Artillery.

Around this time, John McCrae penned his last poem, "The Anxious Dead," which was published in *The Spectator*. The publishers of *The Spectator* must have sorely regretted rejecting "In Flanders Fields."

"The Anxious Dead" was similar in theme to "In Flanders Fields." It certainly had a current of anxiety running through it, as indeed the war was going badly for the Allies at the specific time he wrote it:

The Anxious Dead

O guns, fall silent till the dead men hear
Above their heads the legions pressing on:
(These fought their fight in time of bitter fear,
And died not knowing how the day had gone.)

O flashing muzzles, pause, and let them see
The coming dawn that streaks the sky afar;
Then let your mighty chorus witness be
To them, and Caesar, that we still make war.

Tell them, O guns, that we have heard their call,
That we have sworn, and will not turn aside,
That we will onward till we win or fall,
That we will keep the faith for which they died.

Bid them be patient, and some day, anon,
They shall feel earth enwrapt in silence deep;
    Shall greet, in wonderment, the quiet dawn,
    And in content may turn them to their sleep.

On July 31, 1917, General Douglas Haig launched the Third Battle of Ypres, or Passchendaele, as the Canadians called it. It began with a ferocious bombardment that was supposed to wreak havoc on the German defences. What it mainly did was destroy the simple but effective drainage system that Flemish farmers had used for centuries on their flat fields. That, coupled with one of the wettest years in memory, created a morass of sodden fields that was ultimately as lethal as quicksand.

In one of the early artillery actions of the battle, Lieutenant Revere Osler and eighteen of his mates had a German shell explode in their midst. Revere's chest, thigh, and stomach wounds were severe, and he was transported first to Essex Farm, which by 1917 was a busy dressing station, and finally farther west to No. 47 Casualty Clearing Station (CCS). Harvey Cushing happened to be nearby at No. 46 CCS, at Proven, a western Flemish town. He came as soon as he could but, sadly, there was nothing to be done, and Edward Revere Osler died on August 30, 1917.

It hardly needs to be said that his parents were devastated. Sir William had lost his beloved "Ike" (his nickname for his son) and was inconsolable; he never recovered. McCrae was heartbroken as well, and one wonders if he suffered any guilt over his encouragement of Revere, or at least the example he set in his enthusiastic support of the war effort. Revere was an adult and made his own choice, but that didn't change the sorrow his loved ones felt felt over his loss.

The nightmarish battle known as Passchendaele ground on for weeks. Wooden "duck-boards" were created as sidewalks over the mud. If anyone, man or beast, skidded off them into the muck, the result could be fatal. Men, horses, and mules, sometimes barely wounded or not wounded at all, slipped into the mud and sank slowly to their deaths.

In his book *Ghosts Have Warm Hands*, author Will Bird writes about the Battle of Passchendaele in a telling, understated way:

> Captain Arthur was kind to us. He stood and gazed at our pitiful ranks, gazed without speaking, and I saw in his eyes things of which no man speaks—the things that words would kill. We had a little drill, but rested and slept and had good food until finally we were more like human beings. But every man who had endured Passchendaele would never be the same again, was more or less a stranger to himself.

No. 3 received increasing casualties, including shell wounds, machine-gun injuries, and gas cases. On one occasion, a British soldier came in on the same stretcher as his big, black mongrel dog, Windy; they'd both been wounded in the same infantry advance. The soldier had severe multiple wounds, and Windy had a compound fracture of a rear leg. Windy already had two gold braids on his collar to indicate wounds he'd received in Gallipoli. This would be his third wound stripe.

McCrae set the dog's leg, and he went about in a plaster cast. He was still devoted to his master, but the soldier recovered sufficiently to be shipped to England for convalescence. The authorities would not allow Windy to go with him due to quarantine constraints. Everyone, even Colonel Elder, now acting head of No. 3, pled Windy's case, to no avail. Eventually, the tearful soldier was shipped off, and Windy attached himself tightly to John McCrae. Windy made good friends with Bonneau, and once his leg recovered completely, went off on jaunts with Bonfire, too. But Windy had a couple of troubling traits. He disliked anyone not in khaki, and would bite. McCrae was too busy to supervise him at all times, and the dog soon ran afoul of someone who was most likely not in the military, since the dog was always partial to soldiers.

In early January, 1918, Windy stopped eating and began vomiting continuously. McCrae's fellow pathologist, Lawrence Rhea, thought the cause was poison. Colonel Elder found Jack McCrae and Windy on the floor in McCrae's tent, beside the stove. Windy licked McCrae's hands as he gave the dog morphine until Windy succumbed to the poison and died. The dog was given full military honours and buried on the grounds. "How one hates to lose the faithful beasts!" McCrae lamented in a letter to Dr. Maude Abbott in Montreal on January 9, 1918.

In McCrae's state of mind, this was just one more tragedy he would have to bear, and not a minor one. On

January 6, Major Harvey Cushing, now of No. 13 Royal Army Medical Corps Hospital in Boulogne, came by to visit. Cushing wrote of the visit later in his book *From A Surgeon's Journal*:

> A long tramp in rain and slush up to No. 3 Canadian by roundabout back roads. Tea with Elder and Rhea. John McCrae comes in late: back from giving a lecture in the Lens region. Does not appear to me at all like the "In Flanders Fields" person of former days. Silent, asthmatic, moody.

9

The Death of
an Icon

ON WEDNESDAY, January 23, 1918, Colonel Elder found McCrae asleep in his chair in the officers' mess. This was most unlike him. Elder inquired as to how he was feeling, and McCrae replied that he had a headache and was afraid he may have eaten something that upset his stomach. Colonel Elder suggested he go to bed if he was unwell, which he did. He never got up again.

Elder checked on him at dinnertime, and McCrae said he would stay in bed as he'd had a severe spell of vomiting. McCrae was convinced he'd feel better in the morning if he didn't eat anything and stayed in bed. Other than aching legs, like one gets with the flu, his vital signs seemed normal. He had his normal asthma cough, but otherwise seemed okay. Still, Colonel Elder asked a nursing sister to keep an eye on him overnight.

Later that evening, an order came through from the British staff: Lieutenant-Colonel John McCrae was to be appointed Consulting Physician to the British First Army. This appointment was a huge honour, especially for a Canadian. Colonel Elder came to McCrae's room and read him the telegram. McCrae was very pleased and expected to leave at the beginning of the following week. He discussed with Elder at length his advice on what was to be done on the pathology side of things once McCrae was gone. Elder told him he would announce McCrae's appointment to everyone in the mess and include a complimentary speech about McCrae and his service to No. 3.

The next morning, Elder looked in on him twice, and he was sound asleep. In the afternoon, McCrae was awake and said he felt better but still didn't feel like eating. But late in the afternoon, there were worrying signs. McCrae sent for Elder and seemed concerned that he may have been developing pneumonia. Colonel Elder had two doctors, Captain Lawrence Rhea and Major Keith Rogers, examine his phlegm, and Lawrence Rhea thought there were signs of pneumococci in it. His temperature had gone up to 100°F, but his pulse and respirations seemed normal.

Colonel Elder put a nurse on duty in McCrae's room and instructed her to check his vital signs every two hours. In the meantime, he called over to No. 14, the British officers' hospital in Wimereux, and asked if the senior physician there, Sir Bertrand Dawson, would come and have a look at Lieutenant-Colonel McCrae. Dawson was a friend of McCrae's, and of the McGill hospital, too. He didn't hesitate to come over and check on his friend. Colonel Elder summoned Dawson without telling McCrae because he knew McCrae would refuse, not wanting special treatment. Dawson couldn't find anything serious either, but suggested they transfer him up the road to No. 14 the following morning. That night his temperature went to 101°F, but he was otherwise not too uncomfortable, except for a headache. He was restless, but finally went to sleep in the early hours of the morning.

Later that morning (Friday), the ambulance came for McCrae, and he was brought to the hospital in Wimereux. That evening, Sir Bertrand called Colonel Elder and told him McCrae was considerably better. He said it was probably an abortive attack of pneumonia, and the vaccine injections McCrae and Rhea had been experimenting with to cure McCrae's asthma must have had a positive effect.

But Saturday afternoon, McCrae's condition worsened. His temperature went up, and Elder thought he looked awful but didn't say anything as he didn't want to upset him. McCrae also developed symptoms of cerebral irritation, and Colonel Elder thought he seemed extremely dull, not at all like his usual alert self. Sunday morning, Dawson phoned Elder and said McCrae had passed a very bad night,

John McCrae's funeral, Wimereux, France, January 29, 1918. (General Currie and General Morrison stand immediately left of Bonfire.) GUELPH MUSEUMS

but seemed to be a little better. Still, the cerebral symptoms—the dullness and inability to fully wake up—were worrying Dawson. He suggested that Colonel Elder and Captain Rhea come to No. 14 and do a blood culture and lumbar puncture. When the two men arrived, they found a shocking change in John McCrae. In a letter to Herbert Birkett, Elder wrote, "We went down at once, but found a most remarkable change. He had developed a right-sided hemiplegia, with Bell's palsy, was quite unconscious, and was in fact, dying, with a pulse I could not count."

Colonel Elder and Captain Rhea didn't do either of the tests because they could see it was pointless. Elder sent for McCrae's old Johns Hopkins colleague, Major Harvey Cushing, from No. 13 RAMC war hospital in Boulogne, to come and see McCrae, as he thought it would be a comfort to Tom McCrae, Jack's brother, who was unable to come. Everyone gave up any hope of recovery, and at 1:30 a.m., January 24, 1918, John McCrae died at the British officers' hospital in Wimereux, France.

In an undated letter written by William Dodge (McCrae's batman) to a Mrs. Matthews, he wrote of McCrae's death:

> Colonel Elder and Colonel McCrae were great old rivals in the medical profession, and had some great arguments at times, but I well remember the night we went to the phone together, to enquire how Colonel McCrae was, and he turned to me with a broken voice, and said, "He is dead Dodge," and we both went away blubbering like two school children. Every morning the Colonel used to visit the stable, and always brought a couple of lumps of sugar for Bonfire, and the morning after his death the old horse suddenly turned to the stable door, about the usual time, and stared, as if he could see him, and whinnied. I have always had a superstitious feeling that a person can always watch over anything he loves, and I felt very bad at the time.

On February 1, 1918, in his detailed, heartfelt letter to Colonel Herbert Birkett, Colonel John Munro Elder wrote of McCrae's death, "This is a correct diary of the awful tragedy that has come upon us, and I cannot, even yet, realize that I shall never see Jack again."

* * *

Preparations began for the largest funeral that had ever been held at No. 3 or No. 14, and indeed, one of the biggest, most impressive funerals in all of the First World War. Among other dignitaries were General Arthur Currie, commander of all four divisions of the Canadian army; McCrae's close friend and commander of all Canadian artillery, General Morrison; and General Dodds, another original 1st Brigade CFA officer McCrae had served with before serving at the hospital. Sir Arthur Sloggett and his staff met them all at the gravesite, and Colonel Elder said he didn't think there was a commanding officer from anywhere in the area who did not attend.

In his February 1 letter to Birkett, Elder wrote, "All the officials here, especially Brig-Gen. [Herbert] Wilberforce, were particularly kind to me, and had sympathy for us in our trouble, and regret at the loss of our friend, was universal."

In all, with officers, nursing sisters, non-commissioned officers, and private soldiers, there were more than five hundred people at Lieutenant-Colonel John McCrae's funeral.

Bonfire, accompanied by two grooms, led the procession decked out in traditional white ribbons, courtesy of Brigadier-General Wilberforce, followed by Sir Bertrand Dawson and Colonel Elder.

The day of the funeral was sunny and spring like, and the mourners did not need their overcoats. In his letter to Birkett, Elder wrote,

John McCrae's batman, William Dodge, and Bonfire, January 29, 1918, Wimereux. GUELPH MUSEUMS

> I felt so thankful that the poet of "Flander's Fields" was lying out there in the bright sunshine in the open space which he loved so well, instead of being cramped in that miserable graveyard of Boulogne, which he hated so much. I know this is only sentiment, but sentiment counts after all in this world-war.

McCrae's autopsy revealed that almost his entire body was septic, especially his brain, heart, and kidneys. Wrote Elder, "He was simply flooded with the poison, and never had a chance from the start. Thank God he suffered none!"

After the shock, grief, and resignation at John McCrae's death, hundreds of letters, articles and eulogies were written on both sides of the Atlantic. Harvey Cushing included the following in his book *From a Surgeon's Journal*:

January 28th, 1918, Boulogne

I saw poor Jack McCrae with Elder at No. 14 General last night—the last time. A bright flame rapidly burning out. He died early this morning. Just made Consulting Physician to the 1st Army—the only Canadian so far to be thus honored. Never strong, he gave his all with the Canadian Artillery during the prolonged Second Battle of Ypres and after, at which time he wrote his imperishable verses. Since those frightful days he has never been his old gay and companionable self, but has rather sought solitude. A soldier from top to toe— how he would have hated to die in bed . . . Was anyone more respected and loved than he? Someone has said that "children and animals followed him as shadows follow other men."

We met at No. 14 General—a brilliant sunny afternoon—and walked the mile or so to the cemetery. A company of North Staffords and many R.A.M.C. orderlies and Canadian sisters headed the procession—then "Bonfire," led by two grooms and carrying the regulation white ribbon, with his master's boots reversed over the saddle—then the rest of us. Six sergeants bore the coffin from the gates, and as he was lowered into his grave there was a distant sound of guns—as though called into voice by the occasion. An admirable prayer by one of the three Padres who officiated. The Staffords, from their reversed arms, fix bayonets, and instead of firing over the grave, as in time of peace, stand at salute during the Last Post with its final wailing note which brings a lump to our throats—and so we leave him.

One of the nursing sisters from No. 3, Isabel Davies, wrote to a friend describing the funeral in detail. The following are excerpts from her long letter:

The Death of an Icon

Tuesday, January 29, 1918

My dear Miss Leaford,

Long before this reaches you, you will know about Col. McCrae's death, at present we simply cannot believe it.

It was all so sudden that it leaves one stunned. We have just come back from the funeral, and a wonderful and impressive ceremony it was. The service was delayed till this afternoon to allow his cousin, (Gough, I think was the name) [it was actually Walter Gow] to come from England and Gen. Morrison, his friend and later O.C. to come from the front. I have never seen such a gathering of military notabilities before in France. It was a great and well deserved tribute to the honour and esteem in which Col McCrae was held.

The funeral procession started from No. 14 Gen. The coffin on a wheeled stretcher (actually a gun limber) pulled by R.A.M.C. men. The coffin covered with the Union Jack and heaped high with flowers (we sent a pillow of violets), his belt and cap, of course immediately following the coffin came his horse "Bonfire," his bridle all laced in white ribbon—no mourning is allowed, and the long boots reversed in the stirrups. Poor Bonfire!—he was a pathetic sight—and seeing him riderless brought home to us more forcibly than anything else that could that Col McCrae had left us. Immediately behind Bonfire came the chief mourners including his cousin, Gen. Morrison, Gen. Dodds, Col. Elder—then the firing party North Staffords, about 50 strong, then the officers, lastly the men.

There were three padres—the Presbyterian Service, a prayer, a short reading from the Bible—then another prayer—the burial prayer bringing in "Dust to dust." There was hardly a dry eye. Poor Col. Elder just put his cap over his face. The firing party went through the form but did not fire—the bugles blew the "Last Post." One hears it every night—but—it was very different this afternoon.

It seemed so unkind to come away and leave him there, but it is a beautiful peaceful hillside, facing the sea. Do you remember his poem "We are the dead"—he little thought at the time of writing "In Flanders Fields" how soon he would be remembered with them—Col. Elder is broken hearted. He looks absolutely crushed—On Wed. last Col. McCrae's orders came through to go to the First Army as a Consultant. It was a great honour to a Canadian, but not more than he deserved. I believe that at dinner in the Mess that evening, Col. McCrae was not present, had gone to bed, not feeling too well—In a little speech, Col. Elder told the officers about Col. McCrae's orders and said such nice things, a warm tribute and an appreciation of him, as a man, a soldier and a physician. So many things have happened in the last four weeks which at the time seemed everyday happenings, but now have a great significance. The official photographer was there, both when the Cortege left No. 14 and at the Cemetery so you will doubtless see the photographs.

I don't think I will ever forget today—We can think of nothing else tonight. I thought you would like to hear a few particulars.—The first time I ever met Dr. McCrae I was at a lecture with you.

Good night—much love
Isabel Davies

A colleague of Isabel Davies, Sister Margaret Woods, wrote to another colleague in Canada about McCrae's death. The affection and respect he had of doctors and nurses alike cannot be overstated.

Of course you remember him as a fine, strong healthy man, young, I can see him yet as he lectured to us, also the quiet sadness of his "good-bye" when he came over here. He joined our hospital in the summer of 1915, a changed man, yes, older in appearance, his heart seemed to be with his friends of his [who] "paid the big price" in the Battle of Ypres.

I believe he knew his own condition, and was prepared for the worst. Several times he has told me that if he ever caught pneumonia he would "peg out" because his chest was very weak.

We only wish we could have done something to show our appreciation, but man like, he did not want to be thought sick, and he has gone never knowing how much we cared.

We miss his familiar face and his cheery stories always something to make us laugh. Poor Miss MacIntosh misses him sadly, she has been in the Pneumonia Hut latest, and Col. McCrae spent a good deal of time on patients there. With his going the last home tie seems gone.

Col. Elder is feeling very sadly, for nights he could not sleep, he feels too, that he is strangely alone, no one to talk things over with. Col. Elder thought of everything that Col. McCrae loved. His horse "Bonfire" was at the burial, all his special friends too, they were broken hearted because he became unconscious so quickly that they could not see him.

All came as we did, because we loved him and wanted to show him this last mark of respect.

General Arthur Currie and Major-General Edward Morrison riding toward the Rhine, November 1918. LIBRARY AND ARCHIVES CANADA

When John McCrae died, things were looking bleak for the Allies. His last poem, "The Anxious Dead," speaks to McCrae's state of mind with almost a sense of despair. How sad that he never lived to know of the war's final hundred days, beginning August 8, 1918. Led by the Canadian Corps commander, General Arthur Currie, with Major-General Edward Morrison at his side, Canada's soldiers became an unstoppable and triumphant force in their drive to help bring an end to the Great War.

10

In Flanders Fields:
The Legacy

JOHN MCCRAE was a brilliant, accomplished, and highly respected pathologist. Sir William Osler said he was "the best physician of his generation." He published papers, co-wrote *A Text-Book of Pathology* with his mentor George Adami, and was invited to join the American Medical Association—a rare honour for a Canadian. But there is no escaping that what he is most remembered for is his immortal poem "In Flanders Fields."

The poem was gradually becoming known by word of mouth by the time of McCrae's death. Major-General Edward Morrison said, "The men have learned it with their hearts, which is quite another thing from committing it to memory." Once it appeared in *Punch*, it really took off.

Several poems were written in response to its publication. Moina Belle Michael, an American professor and humanitarian from Georgia, wrote this one:

We Shall Keep the Faith

Oh! you who sleep in Flanders Fields,
Sleep sweet—to rise anew!
We caught the torch you threw
And holding high, we keep the Faith
With All who died.

We cherish, too, the poppy red
That grows on fields where valor led;
It seems to signal to the skies
That blood of heroes never dies,
But lends a luster to the red
Of the flower that blooms above the dead
In Flanders Fields.

And now the Torch and Poppy Red
We wear in honor of our dead.
Fear not that ye have died for naught;
We'll teach the lesson that ye wrought
In Flanders Fields.

Inspired by McCrae's poem, she also conceived the idea of sewing red cloth poppies as a fundraiser for American First World War veterans to pay for their medical and rehabilitation needs. Thus, the red poppy as an interna-

John McCrae's grave, Wimereux Communal Cemetery, June 2011. SUSAN RABY-DUNNE

tional symbol of war remembrance was born. It enjoyed significant favour in the United States for many years, but eventually disappeared. But in the Commonwealth countries that served in the Great War, it became a standard symbol of war remembrance and has never lost its significance or popularity.

* * *

"In Flanders Fields" is one of the best-loved, most often memorized war poems ever written. Even today, more than a hundred years later, it is recited in schools at memorial services, and at Remembrance Day services in every Commonwealth country.

The poem is not without controversy. McCrae has been accused of writing it for propaganda and recruiting purposes. This is false, although it was certainly used for that purpose in the months after it was written. The poem was written as a spontaneous outpouring of grief and anger over the circumstances that led to its themes: the death, not only of a friend and popular member of McCrae's artillery brigade, but of so many young men in the prime of their lives. He was also angered by the wholesale destruction of Ypres, a medieval city full of civilians, and by the first use of poison gas as a weapon of war.

Setting aside politics and even the reasons for the war itself, the context in which the poem was written *must* be taken into account. John McCrae was not in an armchair somewhere behind the lines when he composed it. He was on the front line of a savage battle that went on for seventeen days with no respite. Although he was in the artillery, which is usually well back of the infantry lines, in this case, McCrae's brigade was the farthest forward artillery brigade, and its men suffered terribly for it.

What this means to soldiers, particularly combat veterans and those close to them, is that the writer "gets it." He well knows the cost and the reality of war. "We are the dead" is not a metaphor. John McCrae, and everyone with him, knew that death was only a hair's breadth away and could come at any second.

The sometimes criticized last verse has even been blamed for helping extend the First World War because of its use for stirring up support for the war and encouraging recruitment. In his book *The Great War and Modern Memory*, the American writer and Second World War veteran Paul Fussell writes that "words like 'vicious' and 'stupid' would not seem to go too far in describing the pro-war propaganda of John McCrae's 'In Flanders Fields.'"

It is as though critics of the last verse think that McCrae, perhaps over an extended period of time, sat and mused and strategized as to how he could create the most effective piece of war propaganda possible, when nothing could be farther from the truth.

The last verse was also spontaneous. It was, in its context, a justifiable flash of anger by the soldier/physician after being a helpless witness to men and horses being asphyxiated by poison gas; to terrorized civilians—women, children, and the elderly, mainly—fleeing the shelling of their city to rubble; and to close friends being cut down in their prime.

Critics often ascribe to this poem great, sweeping effects and intent far beyond the scope of its simple, organic creation. "In Flanders Fields" was, and is, a poem of profound immediacy. That is what makes it powerful. That is why it endures.

Epilogue

MANY READERS OF my book *Bonfire—The Chestnut Gentleman* wondered what became of Bonfire after McCrae's death. (The book tells the story behind the poem "In Flanders Field" from Bonfire's point of view.)

McCrae loved Bonfire, and almost every letter or diary entry he wrote during the war mentions the horse and his antics. In Boulogne, while McCrae worked at the war hospital, the horse became almost as much of a celebrity as the man. Bonfire was a great favourite of soldiers, patients, and nursing sisters at the hospital. He was also loved by the local French children, who called him "Feu d'Artifice," a French interpretation of his name. While the mystery of Bonfire's fate is still unsolved, more information has come to light over the last few years.

On February 5, 1918, McCrae's McGill mentor George Adami, now a Lieutenant-Colonel in the CAMC and ADMS, wrote to Doctor John Todd, who had given Bonfire to McCrae. This was only a few days after McCrae's death.

Epilogue

My dear Todd,

I have just heard from Elder [Lt. Col John Elder, Officer in Charge of Surgery at No. 3 Canadian General Hospital (McGill)], who says, "Will you please ask John Todd if he is there what he would like to have done with Bonfire, as it was he who gave the horse to McCrae. I spoke to MacLennan [Lieutenant-Colonel Bart MacLennan of the 42nd Battalion—Royal Highlanders of Canada, and a cousin of Marjorie Todd] and General Morrison on the day of the funeral about him, and they both wished to know Todd's wishes before we make any arrangements about the disposal of his charger. He will certainly never go into a Remount Depot, because Morrison will see to it that he is sent up to Canadian Corps, unless Todd wishes something else to be done with him, and McCrae thought more of the horse than many a man does of his wife.

The letter is signed by George Adami, and at the bottom of it is a handwritten response from Major J.L. Todd: "I have written to Elder, Bart & General Morrison. Between them Bonfire will be well cared for. If it's possible to have him back, will get him; if not he'll have a good master, probably General Morrison who was one of Jack's friends."

It's clear that McCrae's friends were scrambling to find a safe situation for Bonfire. In another letter from Elder to Todd, Elder writes, "I shall certainly not allow "Bonfire" to be thrown into a Remount Depot. He was a very special pet of McCrae's and as a result, is a pet of the whole hospital here."

Although McCrae's friends may have wanted Bonfire to go to Morrison, Morrison had his own beloved horse, King. Morrison had owned King since 1909 and had trained him specially as an artillery officer's horse. General Morrison was one of only a few men with sufficient rank and "pull" to bring their horses back to Canada after the war. Another famous one was General Arthur Currie, who brought his horse, Brock, back to Ontario.

Morrison retired King to the farm of one of his gunners, outside of Ottawa, where he stayed for the rest of his life. It seems likely from this fact that Morrison may also have intervened to keep Bonfire safe for his dear friend Jack McCrae. One likely scenario is that Morrison would have secretly arranged for Bonfire to be retired (which was against army regulations) and probably paid a French farmer to keep the horse safe and well cared for, hopefully to the end of his days. This would explain the lack of information on the subject from people who should have known about Bonfire's postwar fate. They were keeping quiet about it.

At the time of the First World War, Canada had a population of about eight million people; of these, about six hundred thousand men went to war. Approximately sixty-six thousand of those were killed. Hundreds of thousands more returned with catastrophic injuries: missing limbs, parts of faces blown away, burnt, ruined lungs from inhaling poison gas, and other disfiguring wounds.

Epilogue

Then there was shell shock, which didn't get a proper diagnosis until the 1980s, when it was identified as post-traumatic stress disorder (PTSD). We know now that PTSD is caused by prolonged periods of intense fear, extremes of violence, as in hand-to-hand combat, and even witnessing acts of violence. The pervasive din of shellfire in the First World War trenches would certainly have contributed to it. One aspect of PTSD that has only recently been recognized is "moral injury." To be forced to do or see something that is an affront to one's moral centre or one's sense of decency can cause PTSD, even in the most so-called "just war."

It's hard to know all of the after-effects of the First World War with any certainty, or how they shaped the character of our nation. We can never know how many suicides there were, or suicides mistakenly called accidents, or rates of alcoholism or other addictions engaged in by veterans to keep the demons at bay, all or any of which could be directly attributable to the war experience.

The obvious costs can be seen in the hundreds of British Commonwealth military cemeteries, or the hundreds of thousands of names of the missing engraved on monuments like the Menin Gate in Ypres or Thiepval near the Somme battlefields in France. The hidden costs should be remembered too, such as the lasting effect of war on the minds and souls of men who were never the same when they returned. They are the "invisible wounds" that Will Bird speaks of in his book *Ghosts Have Warm Hands*, inflicted on men who were more or less strangers to themselves forevermore.

Although John McCrae died of illness, his service in the First World War killed him as surely as bullets or shells killed other soldiers.

Acknowledgements

I WISH TO THANK Bev Dietrich and Kathleen Wall at Guelph Museums for all their help over ten years of research; Tim Cook at the Canadian War Museum in Ottawa for giving generously of his time whenever I popped in; Piet Chielens at In Flanders Fields Museum in Ieper, Belgium, for his generosity with images; Steve Clifford for his amazing photographs of survivors of the Battle of Kitcheners Wood from the scrapbook of 16th Battalion Canadian Scottish soldier John Denholme (in ten years I have never seen a single photograph of Canadian soldiers during the 2nd Battle of Ypres, only paintings and illustrations); Chris Lyons and Lily Szczygiel at the Osler Library at McGill University, Montreal, Quebec; John Frederick at University of Victoria; and Michael Dorosh, canadiansoldiers.com, for the map of the Ypres Salient in the Great War.

I'm also grateful for all the fascinating friends I've made and kept on the both sides of the Atlantic during this journey of research.

Selected Bibliography

Adami, J.G. *The War Story of the C.A.M.C., 1914–1915, Volume I.* London, UK: Colour Ltd., 1918.

Amery, L.S. *Days of Fresh Air: Being Reminiscences of Outdoor Life.* London, UK: Hutchinson & Co. Ltd., 1940.

Bird, Will. *Ghosts Have Warm Hands.* Ottawa: Clark, Irwin & Company, 1968.

Bliss, Michael. *William Osler: A Life in Medicine.* Toronto: University of Toronto Press, 1999.

Cook, Tim. *At the Sharp End: Canadians Fighting The Great War, 1914–1916, Volume One.* Toronto: Viking Canada, 2008.

———. *Shock Troops: Canadians Fighting The Great War, 1917–1918, Volume Two.* Toronto: Viking Canada, 2008.

Cosgrave, Lawrence Moore. *Afterthoughts on Armageddon: The Gamut of Emotions Produced by the War, Pointing a Moral That Is Not Too Obvious.* Toronto: S.B. Gundy, 1919.

Cushing, Harvey. *From a Surgeon's Journal, 1915–1918.* Boston: Little, Brown and Company, 1936.

———. *The Life of Sir William Osler—Complete in One Volume.* London, UK: Oxford University Press, 1940.

Dancocks, Daniel. *Welcome to Flanders Fields: The First Canadian Battle of the Great War—Ypres, 1915.* Toronto: McClelland and Stewart, 1988.

Fetherstonhaugh, R.C. *No. 3 Canadian General Hospital (McGill), 1914–1919.* Montreal: The Gazette Printing Company, 1928.

Bibliography

Fussell, Paul. *The Great War and Modern Memory*. Oxford: Oxford
University Press, 1975.

Goldbloom, Alton. *Small Patients: Autobiography of a Children's
Doctor*. Montreal: Lippincott, 1959.

Graves, Dianne. *A Crown of Life: The World of John McCrae*. St.
Catharines, ON: Vanwell Publishing Limited, 1997.

Greenfield, Nathan M. *Baptism of Fire: The Second Battle of Ypres and
the Forging of Canada, April 1915*. Toronto: HarperCollins, 2007.

Macphail, Andrew. *In Flanders Fields: An Essay in Character*. Toronto:
William Briggs, 1919.

Mann, Susan (ed.). *The War Diary of Claire Gass, 1915–1918*. Montreal
and Kingston: McGill-Queen's University Press, 2000.

Morrison, E.W.B., Major-General Sir. Unpublished Manuscript of His
Entire Experience in World War One. Courtesy Shaun and John
Fripp. Ottawa, 1920.

———. *With the Guns in South Africa*. Ottawa: Eugene Ursual, 1901.

Archival Materials

Dodge, William. Letter to Mrs. Matthews, undated. McCrae House
Museum, Guelph, ON.

Elder, John Munro. Letter to Herbert Birkett, Boulogne, France, 1st
February, 1918. McCrae House Museum, Guelph, ON.

John McCrae Collection. MG 30 D 209, National Archives of Canada,
Ottawa.

Index

Index

About the Author

SUSAN RABY-DUNNE is an author, military historian, composer, professional speaker, tour guide, and perennial student. She is passionate about international travel and learning about other cultures, and has ridden motorcycles extensively across North America and Europe for forty years.

John McCrae: Beyond Flanders Fields is Susan's fourth book and her second book about John McCrae. *Bonfire: The Chestnut Gentleman* (2012) tells the story behind the poem "In Flanders Fields" from the perspective of McCrae's charger, Bonfire. *Hope in the Colour of Orange: Dutch Civilian Memories of War and Liberation* (2011) is a collection of stories assembled by Susan's writers' group, Monday Morning Writers Group (MMWG).

Susan is on the board of directors and is the Canadian representative of the American charity Soldier's Heart, a community-based organization devoted to healing veterans and their families from war trauma. Learn more at susanrabydunne.com.